How to be Outstanding in the Classroom

Every teacher wants to be outstanding. But what does outstanding mean? And how do we stay outstanding if the goalposts move?

In *How to be Outstanding in the Classroom*, bestselling author Mike Gershon presents you with everything you need to know to make outstanding learning happen in your classroom. The book breaks down the nature of outstanding teaching so as to expose the underlying principles which hold true across the curriculum. Featuring advice on all the different elements that contribute to outstanding teaching and learning including assessment, differentiation, literacy, leadership and ensuring progress, it covers:

- cultivating the habits of outstanding learning;
- the role assessment plays in planning learning, securing progress and helping students to achieve great outcomes;
- leadership and your role as a leader;
- the communication that takes place in the classroom.

Firmly rooted in the day-to-day experiences of being in the classroom, the book clearly explains the why, the how and what to do if things go wrong. Packed full of clear, easy-to-implement strategies and ideas, it is the text you can call upon time and again in order to cultivate and sustain the habits, actions and thoughts of outstanding teaching.

Mike Gershon is a teacher, trainer, writer and educational consultant. He is the author of twenty-one books on teaching, learning and education, and the creator of some of the world's most popular online teaching and learning tools. His resources have been viewed and downloaded more than 2.8 million times by teachers in over 180 countries and he also writes regularly on pedagogy for the *Times Educational Supplement*. Find out more and get in touch at www. mikegershon.com.

D0322687

How to be Outstanding in the Classroom

Raising achievement, securing progress and making learning happen

Mike Gershon

Routledge
Taylor & Francis Group

LONDON AND NEW YORK

First published 2015
by Routledge
2 Park Square, Milton Park, Abingdon, Oxon OX14 4RN

and by Routledge
711 Third Avenue, New York, NY 10017

Routledge is an imprint of the Taylor & Francis Group, an informa business

British Library Cataloguing in Publication Data
A catalogue record for this book is available from the British Library

Library of Congress Cataloging in Publication Data
Gershon, Mike.
How to be outstanding in the classroom : raising achievement,
securing progress and making learning happen / Mike Gershon.
pages cm.
1. Teaching. 2. Learning, Psychology of. 3. Academic achievement.
I. Title.
LB1025.3.G437 2015
371.102–dc23
2014029292

ISBN: 978-1-138-82441-6 (hbk)
ISBN: 978-1-138-82451-5 (pbk)
ISBN: 978-1-315-73358-6 (ebk)

Typeset in Celeste and Optima
by Florence Production Ltd, Stoodleigh, Devon, UK

MIX
Paper from
responsible sources
FSC   FSC® C013056
www.fsc.org

Printed and bound in Great Britain by
TJ International Ltd, Padstow, Cornwall

Contents

1

Introduction

Getting to grips with outstanding

Welcome to *How to be Outstanding in the Classroom*. It's great to have you with us.

This book is all about what it means to be an outstanding teacher, how we go about making outstanding learning happen, and what we need to do to facilitate outstanding progress for our students.

The aim is to present a set of principles – translated into practical habits – which transcend current frameworks of inspection. In so doing, they remain relevant over time.

These are the aspects of outstanding teaching which do not come and go as fashions change. They are the underlying principles which inform and structure outstanding teaching. They are the ways of thinking and acting – the pedagogical skills – that animate great teachers.

We are interested here in unlocking the path to success for every teacher, no matter who they are or what subject they are teaching.

Our aim is not to parrot what current inspection frameworks say. This would be no good because those frameworks are open to change. Instead, we will draw out the principles which underpin the frameworks – and which have underpinned frameworks of the past as well.

In short, we will provide a clear guide as to what you need to do as a teacher in order to be outstanding, to teach outstanding lessons and to make outstanding learning happen. This will be relevant to you today and well into the future.

The book as a whole retains a practical focus. This is important because teaching is, at root, a practical art. While we will make reference to theory and research, we will be sure to couch everything in practical terms.

Doing this means you will have the tools and understanding you need to make the ideas in this book a reality.

The book is a practical manual on which you can call time and again in order to cultivate and sustain the habits, actions and thoughts of outstanding teaching.

It's going to be a good journey.

Outline of the book

Before we move on and start looking at what outstanding actually means, let us attend briefly to the contents of the book.

The remainder of this chapter will reconceptualise outstanding in the context of the classroom, drawing out the principles of outstanding teaching and connecting these to learning.

Chapter 2 will look at the habits of outstanding teaching. It will present seven of these, working through each one in turn and identifying why they constitute such an important part of what you do in the classroom. Each habit will be further explained in its own, individual chapter.

Chapter 3 will spin the focus around and ask, 'What is outstanding learning?' In this chapter we will look at the five habits of outstanding learning. Those things we want all our pupils to be doing, day-in and day-out. We will illustrate the vital link between outstanding teaching and outstanding learning. We need both if we want to be really successful and if we want to secure the very best outcomes for our students.

Chapter 4 takes on the first habit of outstanding teaching by looking at assessment. Here we will consider assessment in the round, thinking about the role assessment plays in planning learning, securing progress and helping students to achieve great outcomes.

Chapter 5 moves on to look at planning in more detail. It takes its lead from the things we look at in Chapter 4 and expands on these in order to present a detailed sense of what outstanding planning looks like. Needless to say, and like every chapter, there will be plenty of practical advice and guidance throughout.

Chapter 6 is all about differentiation: the things you can do to personalise learning in your classroom. The premise here is simple. If you can tailor learning so that it closely matches the needs of your students, good things will ensue. In the chapter we will consider personalisation in terms of assessment, planning, in-lesson and, also, how to help students personalise learning for themselves.

Chapter 7 turns the focus away from the pupils and on to you, the teacher. Here we examine an often over-looked habit; namely, the development of expertise. Expertise is an extremely important factor in the genesis and maintenance of outstanding teaching. And we don't just mean subject knowledge expertise. We will also look at pedagogy, psychology and your knowledge about the students you teach.

Chapter 8 considers leadership and your role as a leader in your own classroom. Here we will examine the nature of leadership, illustrating the importance of the teacher being a leader of their students and of the learning. We will connect together the concepts of leadership and teaching, demonstrating how success in the former is very often linked to familiarity with the latter. We will make connections between leadership in the classroom and the points discussed in Chapters 2 and 3.

In Chapter 9 we turn our attention to literacy, demonstrating how it underpins every subject on the curriculum and, therefore, all outstanding teaching. By breaking literacy down into its component parts – speaking, listening, reading and writing – we will recon-ceptualise the term, making it easier to use and apply. Following on from this, we will look at what it means to be an outstanding literacy teacher, regardless of whether you teach English or not.

This will be supplemented by a section focusing on the connection between literacy and progress.

Our penultimate chapter provides a space in which we can explore the communication which takes place in the classroom, both teacher–student and student–student. We will examine the two most important aspects of this communication: explaining and questioning. Regarding the former, we will look at the importance of providing students with ways of accessing and assimilating new content. In terms of the latter, we will focus on the way in which effective questioning (by teachers and students) is central to securing significant progress across the board.

Our final chapter will be a conclusion, drawing together the themes of the book. Here we will pose the question: Who do you want to be? This will help you to reflect on what outstanding teaching means to you. It will also encourage you to positively visualise the teacher – the *outstanding* teacher – you want to be.

So there we have it! Outstanding teaching broken down and explained in a series of easy-to-follow, practical steps. It may be that you want to skip ahead to individual chapters which spark your interest. Please feel free.

Personally, I would suggest reading this introduction first, followed by Chapters 2 and 3. This will provide you with a clear sense of what we are trying to achieve in the book. You can then read Chapters 4 to 10 in whatever order you wish. While they are sequenced logically, they are also self-contained in the sense that they each focus on a different habit of outstanding teaching.

With all that said, let us begin.

What is outstanding?

The word 'outstanding' has come to be associated with great teaching due to the Ofsted school inspection grading system used to classify the quality of schools in the United Kingdom.

At the time of writing, this grading system has four categories. The top two of these are 'Good' and 'Outstanding'. These grades are assigned to different aspects of a school such as quality of teaching and the achievement of pupils. The school is then given an overall grade linked to the individual grades it receives.

Traditionally, lesson observations conducted internally to a school – those done for performance management – have used the Ofsted grading categories in order to reach judgements about the quality of a lesson. As such, individual lessons come to be judged as 'Good', 'Outstanding' and so on. This often leads to situations where a teacher is assigned the epithet their lesson has received. Thus we hear of 'good teachers' and 'outstanding teachers'.

We can see that the word 'outstanding', while having a common meaning in the English language, also has a specific meaning within the professional context of teaching. This meaning is informed by the nature of Ofsted school inspections, the past history of the inspection system and the attendant political and professional discussions which surround them.

In the first sense then, outstanding is whatever Ofsted say it is. This might be said explicitly or it might be inferred through their identification of outstanding practice.

However, this is not hugely helpful to us.

Two specific problems throw themselves up:

– What if the Ofsted framework changes?
– Isn't there a more solid foundation for defining outstanding in the context of teaching and learning?

Fortunately, there is. And this is what we will delineate in this book.

This more solid foundation is actually predicated on the principles which underpin inspections and which guide schools and system leaders across the country in trying to secure the very best educational experiences for the millions of children who move through primary and secondary schools year after year.

In one sense, outstanding teaching is teaching which stands out. This point plays on the common definition of the word; the one with which we are all familiar and which informs our use of 'outstanding' when we are communicating on a day-to-day basis.

But it is important to note that to stand out does not, by necessity, imply exclusivity. In one reading it might do – the situation in which we have a stand-out candidate, for example, whose qualities are such that they prevent anybody else from securing the job.

In the context of teaching outstanding lessons and facilitating outstanding learning, exclusivity does not have any part to play. Clearly, if it did, things would be in a parlous state. Imagine the situation if judgements of outstanding were apportioned based on a system of percentages, or if they were assigned from a box containing only a limited number of top-level judgements.

Such an approach would in fact militate against outstanding teaching and learning. This is because it would send out the message that the one thing everybody wants to achieve is in fact only accessible by a pre-defined minority.

Outstanding teaching and learning can be achieved in any classroom, by any teacher, at any time and in any place. It can be found in isolated pockets within a school or it can sweep across an entire institution. There is no limit – none whatsoever – to the extent of outstanding teaching and learning.

This is because, as we will set out to show below, outstanding teaching and learning is based on underlying principles which can be understood, internalised and followed by any teacher.

The only things you need are this book, targeted effort and a belief that you can change and grow.

If you are in possession of all three – and these are three things which everybody can possess – then you are half-way towards achieving your goal of being outstanding. And, by extension, giving your pupils the very best chance possible of achieving great things.

Before we move on to describe and define these principles to which we have been referring, let me make one final point.

Superb education has existed for centuries, even thousands of years. For much of that time it has been found in tiny sections of society and has benefited exceptionally small numbers of people. The challenge today – indeed the challenge that has been with us since the advent of the Industrial Revolution and the subsequent changes to society this brought about – is to secure and embed the highest possible standards of education throughout a national system.

In short, we are seeking to give everybody who attends a school the very best education possible.

Seeing as how education, at root, is formed from the interactions which take place between teacher and student – or the interactions the teacher facilitates between different students – it seems safe to say that teaching and learning is, and always will be, at the core of what we are trying to achieve.

This fact is a central theme of the book.

Ultimately, and as you no doubt well appreciate, it is teaching and the facilitation of learning which brings results. Other measures – administration, reform of the curriculum, changes to school structures – may have some impact but, beyond all this, there is always to be found, at the heart of it all, the interplay between student and teacher.

This truth is perhaps not fashionable. Nor does it fit necessarily with the aims and intentions of politicians and leaders (though, at times it does). Yet it is one we all know instinctively through our own experiences. And it is one which history teaches us from the time of the Ancient Greeks onwards.

In the Dialogues of Plato, those foundation stones of Western thought, we see a teacher – Socrates – helping his students to grow and to develop their minds through what he says and through what he does. This is what teaching is all about.

It is what outstanding teaching is all about: the interactions between you and your pupils.

It is what we will illustrate time and again throughout the course of this book.

The principles of outstanding teaching

Now we come to the principles, those things which underpin inspection frameworks, which bind our notions of what we ought to do in the classroom into a whole, which animate the decisions, choices and judgements outstanding teachers make on a daily basis.

Here they are:

- Progress is key.
- Intelligence is not fixed.
- Everybody has the capacity to learn, to focus and to expend targeted effort.
- Literacy is every teacher's job.
- Pace and challenge are a permanent feature.
- Repetition is not to be eschewed.
- Feedback is vital.
- Relationships need to be built and sustained.
- Learning is at the heart of everything else.

Simple!

All these points would underpin any inspection framework worth its salt. They would also underpin the work of any outstanding teacher. You simply can't be outstanding without following most, if not all, these principles, whether you are doing it knowingly or not.

Let us now look at each one in turn.

Progress is key

Progress is what teaching is all about. If our students don't make progress, they haven't learned anything. If they don't make progress, we need to seriously question what we are doing and whether it is truly meeting their needs. We might also, in some situations, need to question their behaviour and application. After all, students need to be receptive to the possibility of learning at the very least before we can hope to secure progress for them.

In any learning endeavour, progress is the goal. This applies to driving, cooking and playing sport just as much as it applies to life in the classroom. If we do not make progress, learning is not happening.

Outstanding teaching involves facilitating significant learning gains for all students. This is self-evident. In this book, we will illustrate various ways through which you can make this happen.

Intelligence is not fixed

Believing this fact – and in the process denying the reach of the pernicious myth which suggests otherwise – means operating from the premise that every student you teach is in a position to make progress, regardless of their starting point.

If you do not accept this principle, then you are not in a position to secure significant progress across the board. This is because you will be labouring under the false assumption that intelligence is a genetic inheritance which cannot be altered through the efforts of the individual.

We know that it can be altered, however. We know that intelligence can be grown, developed and cultivated. We know that the mind is like the body – it can be trained.

How do we know this? Scientific research such as that carried out by Carol Dweck, among others. Anecdotal evidence wherein people we know or people we are familiar with through the media explain how they have grown and changed over time. And, logical deduction: we do not end up the way we began. Therefore, change can happen. We all learn things from the moment we are born. Therefore we all have the capacity to learn. This means that intelligence is not fixed for any one of us: it can be grown and developed.

Everybody has the capacity to learn, to focus and to expend targeted effort

This principle is closely connected to the previous two. If we accept that progress is key and that intelligence is not fixed, we must also accept that everybody has the capacity to learn. This sounds like an obvious point – what teacher wouldn't believe this? – but, as with all these principles, it is about making the premises which underpin our actions clear; bringing them to the front of our consciousness so that we can use them to inform everything we do.

The second part of this principle – that everybody has the capacity to focus and to expend targeted effort – is perhaps a little more opaque.

By focus we mean the ability to pay active attention to that which we are doing. This ability, inherent to us all, is vitally important if we want to learn and learn well. You can see it most easily by watching very young children learn. A two year old, for example, will focus their entire attention on something new. Watching them, it can feel as if we are looking at a child who is staring into the very core of meaning: boring their way down into the fundamental purpose of the universe.

I exaggerate, of course! The point though is to illustrate the extent to which babies and young children exhibit strong, attentive focus in order to learn. This indicates both its importance and the fact that it is accessible to all of us.

In terms of targeted effort, this is the practical means through which learning happens and, as a corollary, through which significant progress can be secured.

Effort can be exerted by everybody. Effort leads to us acting on the world and on ourselves. If this effort is targeted, it is likely to be most effective. Therefore, targeted effort can lead to great learning gains.

Literacy is every teacher's job

Language allows us to do two things.

First, it allows us to communicate with others. Second, it allows us to communicate with ourselves.

In the first case, this means bridging the gap between minds. It means being able to connect what we think, sense and experience with the thoughts, senses and experiences of other people. Of course, we can communicate without language, but this communication falls a long way short of the rich, deep, broad communication language allows us to access.

In the second case, we are referring to the way in which language acquisition changes our minds. Being able to speak and then, as time passes, being able to read and write, fundamentally changes the way in which we conceptualise ourselves, our relationship to the world and the thoughts that we have. To demonstrate this point, conceive of an individual the same age as you who had never learned to speak or to read or to write. Such a person would have had a very different life. Potentially an extremely difficult, painful life in many respects.

Extrapolating out from these two points we can see that literacy is fundamental to success in school. As teachers we know this fact and we see the consequences of it every day.

We can therefore assume that literacy is everybody's business. If we want our students to do outstandingly well – to make superb progress and to enjoy significant learning gains – then we must attend to literacy. We must accept that part of our jobs, regardless of what we teach, is to help pupils communicate effectively – both in speech and in writing – and to help them to read well.

Pace and challenge are a permanent feature

Pace and challenge are necessary if we want all pupils to make progress and if we want students to learn as much as possible. Without pace, engagement is likely to slide and, with it, the effort that pupils put in will probably wane. Without challenge, students will not be pushed to continue stretching their thinking. Instead, they will remain comfortable with modest learning gains, these being based on a sense of security and maintaining the status quo.

Pace manifests itself as the speed of the lesson. Good pace means students are continually engaged with the learning. It also means that pupils find themselves consistently meeting new ideas or information or being asked to apply ideas and information in different ways, through the course of the session. This principle really focuses on the minutiae of teaching. In so doing, it makes us aware of the fact that every second of every minute of every lesson has an impact on learning.

Challenge is concerned with intellectual stimulation. It does not mean setting the bar exceptionally high lesson after lesson. This may prove counter-productive as it can be demoralising. Rather, it means continually pushing students to think and act at the very edges of what they are capable of. In so doing, they will continually push back those edges, learning and progressing as they go.

Repetition is not to be eschewed

At first glance, this might appear a slightly odd principle to include here. Why draw attention to repetition? Why highlight it as one of the key factors central to outstanding teaching?

Well, the fact of the matter is that repetition can sometimes be overlooked. Regardless of what causes this oversight, it is important that we attend to the benefits of repetition, so that we might come to realise just what a central role it plays in outstanding learning.

Repetition – or practice – allows us to learn, perfect and master skills and ideas. By repeating things over and again, we become more familiar with them. This familiarity allows us to use and manipulate the things in question with greater care and precision.

The best kind of repetition is active practice. That is, practice in which we actively attend to what we are doing and in which we use targeted effort to repeat and improve whatever it is that we are concerned with.

So, to be clear, we are not simply advocating rote learning.

What we are identifying as beneficial is repetition wherein the learner is actively engaged in what they are doing – thinking and reflecting on what is happening to the extent that they come to better understand and better know that with which they are engaged.

For an illustration of this point, look at high-performing sportspeople, famous artists or exceptional writers. In nearly every case, the individual in question has engaged in excessive practice and this practice has involved active thought. It is this which has led them to make such significant learning gains.

Feedback is vital

Feedback is the means through which the teacher communicates to students what it is they need to do in order to make progress.

It is the teacher's opportunity to call on their superior knowledge and experience in order to guide the learner in their development. Feedback is the facilitator of progress over time. Without it, students are likely to make sporadic progress rather than progress which is continuous, directed and relevant.

In addition, feedback is the information pupils need if they are to target their efforts most effectively. Without appropriate feedback, students may target their efforts in ways which are less effective and less helpful than might otherwise be the case.

Outstanding teachers provide students with high-quality feedback on a regular basis. This takes the form of written, verbal and non-verbal feedback. In its written and verbal forms, it will always make clear what it is pupils need to do to succeed.

Furthermore, feedback must be supplemented by time set aside for implementation. If pupils do not have the opportunity to implement their feedback – if feedback is provided in order to tick a box rather than to genuinely facilitate progress – then great learning is unlikely to happen. The benefits of feedback will simply not be brought to bear.

Relationships need to be built and sustained

This principle has been inherent in everything we have said so far and also harks back to the points we made at the end of the last section about teaching being predicated on interactions and the communication (in all its forms) which takes place between students and teachers (and also that which is facilitated by the teacher between students).

Relationships first need to be built. This process of developing rapport, setting boundaries and creating a positive environment for learning is essentially the groundwork all teachers engage in so that they can implement the other principles here enumerated.

They then need to be sustained. This process is concerned with maintaining the focus on learning, positive attitudes and the other features of outstanding learning we have sought to cultivate initially.

Regarding this final point, we should note that, while this book is concerned with outstanding teaching, throughout our analysis we are also looking at what makes outstanding learning and outstanding learners. That is why Chapter 3 is focused on the habits of outstanding learning and learners – with these being presented in tandem, and intimately connected to, the habits of outstanding teaching.

Learning is at the heart of everything else

And so we conclude with our final principle, the one that pretty much sums up everything we are trying to achieve in the classroom.

Sometimes we can forget that learning is at the heart of what we do. We might take it for granted, seeing as how it infuses all our day-to-day work. Drawing attention to it and bringing it to the forefront of our minds helps us to remember the ultimate aim of our jobs; the reason we are employed in the first place; the reason our society places a value on what we do and the system of which we form a part.

As you will note, the preceding eight principles all work together to make outstanding learning happen. As such, you might like to use this ninth and final principle as an overarching concept beneath which to gather and order the other elements which, in total, form the basis for outstanding teaching today and in the future.

Progress, achievement and engagement

We draw this introduction to a close by focusing on two final points.

The first is the centrality of these three words:

progress, achievement and engagement

For me, these three words neatly encapsulate the principles of outstanding teaching, as well as the practical habits which allow you to make this happen. They also indicate the importance of the learner in the process of teaching: their role and the underlying point that outstanding teaching is much more about facilitation than it is about showmanship, all-singing and all-dancing lessons and performing in front of your students.

You can use these three words as a lens through which to view everything you do as part of your planning, teaching and assessment. They will provide you with a shorthand means through which to draw your mind back to the ideas, principles and habits detailed in this book.

As such, they can be thought of as a thinking tool – a memory device – which will help you to continually put into practice the habits and principles of outstanding teaching.

Making learning happen is outstanding teaching

And this is where we conclude our introduction.

A final point to remember as we begin our journey through the habits which will allow you to make the principles a part of your practice, every day of your working life:

Making learning happen is outstanding teaching.

Doing this ensures progress. Which, in turn, raises achievement and secures great outcomes for all the pupils we teach. And that is what all of us want; it is the reason we go into the job in the first place.

So, without further ado, let us look at how we can make this a reality.

2 Cultivating the habits of outstanding teaching

Habits are ways of acting. They are things we do and the things we tend to do again and again over a period of time. If you can get into a good habit, fantastic! That means you will be doing good things repeatedly.

In terms of teaching, we want to cultivate good habits. This will ensure that we are doing the things necessary to raise achievement, to secure progress and to engage learners, week after week, term after term.

The seven habits presented in this chapter are derived from the principles of outstanding teaching we outlined in the introduction. Each one is accompanied by its own chapter later in the book. These chapters provide extensive practical guidance, covering things you can do to make the habits a reality.

Before we turn to the habits themselves, it is worth noting that the inspiration for this approach – this way of thinking – comes from the hugely popular and influential book written by Stephen R. Covey – *The 7 Habits of Highly Effective People* (2004).

In this book, Dr Covey presents an approach to life and work which is principle-centred and designed to be holistic; that is, one which encompasses all aspects of who we are and what we do.

I pass no judgement on the book itself – that I leave to others and to you, should you wish to go out and read it. Suffice to say, what we are adapting here is the way of thinking which it posits.

Namely, that by identifying habits and then seeking to make these habits our own, we find ourselves in a position whereby we can continually make good choices, decisions and judgements which fit in with our overall aims and intentions.

In the context of outstanding teaching then, I am suggesting that by cultivating the seven habits here outlined, you will be in a position to regularly teach outstanding lessons. What is more, you will retain in your mind a series of practices you can use to assess and respond to any situation you encounter.

Thus, you will always be able to make decisions and judgements which tally with your wider aim – to teach outstanding lessons – and the sub-aims which constitute this – raising achievement, securing progress and engaging learners.

Here are the habits:

- *Habit One*: Eliciting and Using Information (see Chapter 4)
- *Habit Two*: Facilitating Progress (see Chapter 5)
- *Habit Three*: Personalising Learning (see Chapter 6)
- *Habit Four*: Building Expertise (see Chapter 7)
- *Habit Five*: Leading Learning (see Chapter 8)
- *Habit Six*: The Lens of Literacy (see Chapter 9)
- *Habit Seven*: Creating Clarity and Confusion (see Chapter 10).

In this chapter we will look at each one in turn, explaining precisely what it means and why it is important. As we will see, some are habits of mind, some are habits of action and some are a mixture of the two.

Habit One: Eliciting and Using Information

This habit is concerned with assessment for learning (AfL). Assessment for learning is a suite of strategies, tools and techniques through which teachers can raise achievement. The approach sees assessment being used to support and encourage learning.

At heart, assessment for learning involves three things:

- Eliciting and using information
- Providing formative feedback
- Opening up success criteria.

We include points two and three elsewhere. Here, we are focused on the first point. That, and that only, is the basis of our first habit.

As an aside, research has shown assessment for learning and the elements of which it is constituted to be a highly effective way through which to raise achievement. To find out more, try reading *Assessment for Learning: Putting it into Practice,* Black et al (2003), *Inside the Black Box,* Black and Wiliam (1990) and *Visible Learning for Teachers,* Hattie (2011).

So, eliciting and using information then. What exactly does this mean?

Well, eliciting information means continually getting information about students' thinking, learning and attitudes.

Using this information means calling on it in order to shape and adapt what you do in the classroom.

As you can see, doing the latter will help you to teach and communicate in a way which more closely matches the needs of your pupils. This will help you to ensure they make progress.

Let us illustrate the point with an example.

Teacher A plans and delivers their lessons without taking account of their students. They seek no information from them and they do not try to ascertain any sense of where they are at or what they know in terms of their learning. Instead, they bludgeon on regardless.

Teacher B plans and delivers lessons which do take account of their students. They are attentive during lessons and when marking books. They see everything as an opportunity to elicit information about students' thinking, learning and attitudes. They then use this information to shape and adapt what they do.

Clearly, the pupils in Teacher B's class have a much greater chance of making sustained progress than the students in Teacher A's class.

We can elicit information about students' learning in all manner of ways – through listening to them, observing them work, talking to them, asking questions, reading and marking their work and so on. In fact, every interaction is an opportunity to elicit useful information.

For example, as pupils walk into the classroom you might observe that they are hot and tired after a long lunch break in the sun. You can use this information to adapt your starter activity, maximising the potential for engagement and immediate learning gains.

On a less prosaic level, you might use a whole-class feedback technique (for more on which, see Chapter 4) to find out whether pupils have understood a particular concept. Having elicited this information you then find yourself in a position to make an informed, useful decision about the lesson: do you move things on, do you revisit the concept or do you split the class up and set students off on different tasks?

As a third example, consider marking pupils' books. Here, you are able to elicit information on an individual level and on a whole-class level. You can use the former to shape and mould your feedback, as well as your individual interactions in the forthcoming lessons. You can use the latter to make judgements about where you are at in terms of your scheme of work and where it would be sensible to move to next.

Eliciting information about students' learning gives you the knowledge you need to adapt and modify your planning, teaching and communication.

Using this information means making practical changes to what you do inside and outside the classroom, based on the needs of your students. If the work is too easy, you can make it harder. If someone has not understood an idea, you can give them more support.

If another pupil needs to change their style of writing, you can give them the necessary feedback.

For the teacher, knowledge is power.

By habitually eliciting information you will find yourself increasingly attuned to the needs of your students. This will allow you to alter what you do so that it meets and even exceeds those needs, facilitating great progress and raising achievement in the process.

Habit Two: Facilitating Progress

Progress means that students learn.

Outstanding progress means they learn a lot. It means they can do more, understand more or know more – often a combination of all three.

Habit Two: Facilitating Progress means having the notion of progress constantly at the forefront of your mind. It means seeing everything that you do through this lens. It involves regularly asking yourself the following questions:

- How is what I am doing helping pupils to make progress?

- What impact will this have on students' progress?

- What can I do here that will help pupils to make better progress?

As you can see, thinking in this way means passing everything you do through a fine sieve. It is a little like making a consommé. At the end, we want something which is as clean and as pure as possible, with all imperfections removed. This gives us a product which is more powerful, more effective and more closely aligned to what we set out to achieve.

Keeping progress at the front of one's mind involves paying attention at all times to the fact that teaching is ultimately about learning and that, to ensure our students do as well as they possibly can, we must always aim to facilitate as much progress as possible.

Cultivating the habits of outstanding teaching

This begins when we plan, carries on while we teach and interact with students and goes right on through to the times during which we mark and assess.

Any impact we can have on students and their learning is tied up in these three points: planning; teaching; marking.

In order to have the biggest impact possible, we must cultivate the habit of viewing what we do through the lens of progress. This will help us to keep learning and achievement at the forefront of our minds.

It will also help us to make excellent decisions. For example, if we are faced with a situation on which we need to decide whether or not we want to keep a certain activity in a lesson, we can ask ourselves a question such as: Is this contributing to the progress my students make?

If the answer is yes, great. We retain the activity. If the answer is no, we change things.

You will note that two things are going on with this particular habit.

First, we are aiming to ensure that everything we do is consistent with securing great progress. Our aim is, first and foremost, to help students to learn. By thinking about progress as we work, we can be certain that this aim remains high on our list of priorities, allowing us to have a significant impact on our students.

Second, we are using the habit as a thinking tool – one through which we can regularly make good decisions that will help us to achieve our aims. In so doing, we bring consistency to our decision-making processes and ensure that we are able to make similar decisions, based on the desire to raise achievement and secure progress, again and again.

It is worth noting here that this habit is, out of all of them, the one most closely associated with lesson planning. This is inevitable as effective lesson planning is an essential prerequisite for the facilitation of progress.

If we do not plan lessons effectively, then students will be in a much worse position when we come to teach them than would otherwise be the case. For this reason, Chapter 5, in which we look at the practical things you can do to make this habit a reality, focuses in large part on lesson planning.

There, we will look at different techniques you can employ to make sure that the lessons you create facilitate progress for all students from beginning to end. Of particular note will be the relevance and use of Bloom's Taxonomy of Educational Objectives. This educational idea is bound up with the notion of mastery learning.

And what is mastery learning if not the securing of continued progress until such a time as we have fully come to terms with the skills or content in question?

For more on Bloom's Taxonomy, see *A Taxonomy for Learning, Teaching, and Assessing,* Anderson et al. (2000) and the original research: *The Taxonomy of Educational Objectives: Book 1 – Cognitive Domain,* Bloom (1965).

Habit Three: Personalising Learning

Personalising learning is more commonly known as differentiation.

Differentiation is all the things you as a teacher can do to ensure that your lessons, your teaching, your planning and your marking meet the needs of your students. The aim here is to ensure that all students can access the learning and make great progress.

As a term, differentiation has a chequered history. It has frequently been applied without first being defined, leading to vague and ambiguous usage. This has led many teachers and leaders to question what it actually means, whether it is plausible to effectively differentiate on a lesson-by-lesson basis and whether there is any clear sense about what differentiation looks like or means in practice.

Here we will allay all these concerns in two swift strokes.

First, the definition.

Cultivating the habits of outstanding teaching

Differentiation is all the things the teacher can do or facilitate which cause students to access the learning and make great progress.

This includes specific support for those who exhibit low ability in the subject and for those who exhibit high ability. It also includes anything which can help any student to gain purchase, come to terms with the work and push themselves to succeed.

Second, matters practical.

In practical terms, differentiation can be divided into five separate categories:

- Activities
- Questioning
- Words and writing
- Things the teacher can do or use
- Things you can ask students to do or use.

Thinking about the concept in this way makes life much easier. This is for a number of reasons.

First, it helps us to contextualise differentiation and to see how we might practically apply it. Second, it allows us to think about the different elements in turn instead of trying to get to grips with what is a large topic in one sitting. Third, it gives us different routes into differentiation, suggesting various ways in which we might personalise learning, with relative ease, regardless of who we are teaching or what we are teaching them.

Now that we have a clearer idea of what differentiation is, it will be helpful to ask and answer the question: Why should we make personalising learning one of our habits?

We will think about this in three ways: first, from the perspective of motivation, second, from the angle of progress and third, from the point of view of equality.

In terms of motivation, we know from our own experience and from the work of psychologists such as Abraham Maslow that motivation is closely tied to our being seen and treated as an individual. Consider the difference between a specific word of thanks from your boss and a blanket message thanking everybody but naming no one.

The former is intrinsically more valuable and more motivational. It has meaning and sense attached to it.

In the context of the classroom, habitually thinking about differentiation means seeing all learners as individuals. In turn, this means finding ways in which we can help and support them individually. This means doing things which are likely to help them to succeed. This success will be a function of them being able to access the work as a result of what we have done. Thus, effective differentiation tends to lead to more motivated and engaged learners.

The corollary of this is that motivated and engaged learners are more likely to make excellent progress. This is self-evident and needs no further explanation. What we should point out, however, is that our second habit saw us paying close attention to the facilitation of progress. Therefore, we can note that personalising learning wherever possible will help us to achieve our other aim of ensuring great progress across the board.

Finally, we come to the issue of equality. This is of philosophical concern.

Given as how it is our job to teach young people, and that all young people possess the same basic right to have access to an education, it becomes incumbent on us to ensure we do as much as possible to help all those pupils we teach achieve as highly as they can. Personalising learning – differentiation – is the number one way we can do this.

Of course, the flipside is that students have the responsibility of coming to school ready and willing to learn. But, that aside, we are the ones in the strongest position to ensure everyone has the opportunity to learn and to learn as much and as effectively as possible.

For more insight into differentiation, take a look at *Teaching Today* by Geoff Petty (2009) and my own book *How to use Differentiation in the Classroom: The Complete Guide* (2013).

Habit Four: Building Expertise

Our next habit takes the focus away from the students for a moment and plants it firmly on you, the teacher.

It concerns your own expertise.

In terms of a habit, this means continually looking to build, develop and grow your own expertise.

And it should be pointed out here that your expertise covers at least four different yet equally important categories:

- Subject knowledge
- Pedagogy
- Psychology
- Knowledge of the students you teach.

Before we look at each of these in a little more detail, let us examine why we have identified building your expertise as one of our seven habits.

In the classroom, you are the professional. It is you who has trained to do the job, you who has chosen to focus your time and energy on becoming a teacher. As such, you have entered into one of the social contracts our society offers to all of us fortunate enough to find employment: the division of labour.

The division of labour means that different people become specialists at different things. This allows society to achieve much more than would be possible if everyone had to do a multitude of different roles. So, for example, the farmer farms, the builder builds and the teacher teaches. This process sees people becoming specialists.

Specialisation brings with it the development of expert knowledge and understanding. Through this expertise, each of us who finds ourselves part of the division of labour is in a position to put their skills to use in order to do a better job than someone else who is less expert.

In the context of teaching, it means that we are the teaching experts. We are the ones whose job it is to be experts and who can be expected to use this expertise in order to help students to make as much progress as possible.

With that in mind, let us return to our four areas of expertise.

Subject knowledge comes first. This could be highly specialised if we are a secondary school teacher or it could be more general yet also broader if we work in a primary school. Either way, we will possess the knowledge necessary to teach that which forms part of the curriculum.

Next is pedagogy. This concerns the art of teaching – all those things we do which help us to plan and teach brilliant lessons; the practical strategies, activities and techniques we use in the classroom; as well as the theoretical knowledge and scientific research we make use of as part of our teaching.

After this comes psychology. Expertise here varies considerably from teacher to teacher. Most members of the profession will have a good working knowledge of the psychology of the age groups they teach. This comes through experience. A good proportion of teachers will also have invested time in understanding wider psychological issues such as motivation and learning theory. Finally, some teachers will have given thought to the insights of developmental and cognitive psychology as they relate to life in the classroom.

Finally, we come to the expertise which is highly specific to individual teachers: their knowledge and understanding of the pupils they teach. This expertise is closely connected to Habit One: Eliciting and Using Information. Through eliciting information about students, their learning, their thinking and their attitudes, teachers are in a position to become experts about the pupils they teach (in the context of the classroom).

Where does all this leave us?

Well, first we can point to the fact that teachers have at least four important areas of expertise and that the knowledge and understanding which flows from these areas places teachers in a strong position to raise achievement, secure progress and engage their students.

Second, we can note that every teacher who wants to be outstanding should get into the habit of growing and developing this expertise – in all the areas – such that they might have more to offer their pupils and more on which to call while they are doing their jobs.

That you are reading this book indicates your agreement, at least in part, with this point. It also suggests that you have already begun to cultivate the fourth habit and are in a strong position from which to move off and develop it further.

For more on the relevance and importance of expertise, have a look at recently published briefings and reports on teacher effectiveness by the Sutton Trust, the Bill and Melinda Gates Foundation and Rand Education:

- 'Improving the impact of teachers on pupil achievement in the UK' – interim findings, the Sutton Trust, September 2011, www.suttontrust.com/researcharchive/improving-impact-teachers-pupil-achievement-uk-interim-findings/

- 'Teachers Matter: Understanding Teachers' Impact on Student Achievement' – Rand Education report on the impact of teachers, www.rand.org/content/dam/rand/pubs/corporate_pubs/2012/RAND_CP693z1–2012–09.pdf

- The Bill and Melinda Gates Foundation report on the measures of effective teaching, www.metproject.org/.

Habit Five: Leading Learning

In habit five we see the focus staying with you the teacher but also shifting back onto the students at the same time. Here we are thinking about how you can be a leader in the classroom. We are concerned with what you can do, say and think, which will see you leading the learning that your students are engaged in.

The importance of this cannot be overstated.

In any classroom, the teacher is the professional. They are the person whose job it is to take charge, to facilitate, to teach and to lead. Through doing this they make learning happen.

Through doing this they secure great progress and raise achievement.

Outstanding teaching necessarily involves the teacher taking hold of this fact and running with it to the extent that they are leading everything which goes on in their classroom.

This does not mean that they are the centre of attention at all times. Far from it.

Instead, it means that they are managing and controlling the environment such that it is conducive to learning happening and to this learning being as effective as possible and of the highest standard possible.

In order to illustrate how leadership of learning plays out in practice, let us imagine a situation in which there is no leadership.

In such a classroom the following is likely to exist:

- There will not be a clear sense of purpose. Pupils will struggle to see the wider point of what they are doing.

- Students may well feel demotivated. They will lack the intrinsic motivation which is necessary for success and which great teachers cultivate through their leadership.

- The atmosphere may not be particularly focused on learning.

- There will not be a clear sense of direction regarding the learning or regarding who is in charge and where they are taking the class.

- Across the board, students will not be achieving what they are capable of. Some may be achieving well but, overall, pupils will be operating below their potential.

Cultivating the habits of outstanding teaching

Leadership is about taking people to places they can't or won't go themselves. It is about staking out the path, showing people the way and then equipping them with the tools, skills and knowledge they need to get there.

As you will have no doubt noted by now, all the other habits contribute to your leading the learning. Each one requires you to be in charge, to guide your students forwards and to do the things necessary to ensure they can make as much progress as possible.

Outstanding teachers not only lead the learning that goes on in their classroom, but they also help their pupils to become leaders in their own right.

This is about developing habits of mind in our students that will help them to be successful both in the classroom and beyond. We will look at these points in more detail in the next chapter when we consider the five habits of outstanding learning.

Here, we will attend to two specific points: independent learning and growth mindsets.

Independent learning is important because, ultimately in life, it is the individual's actions that, in general, shape what happens to them – what they achieve and how far they get. If we can inculcate this understanding in our students, and if we can lead them in such a way that they develop the habits of independent learning and thinking, then we will be doing them a great service.

We will be preparing them for life outside of school, giving them the tools they will need to be successful, no matter what path they decide to take.

Growth mindsets (see the work of Carol Dweck) refer to the way in which we perceive our own skills and abilities. If we have a growth mindset, then we believe that our skills and abilities are not fixed and that we can change, grow and develop them over time through our own efforts.

As with independent learning, this is a habit of mind we want our students to develop. As with independent learning, it is a habit which we can lead them to internalise through the way in which we act, speak and think when we are in the classroom.

For more on the importance and relevance of leadership, have a look at *The Score Takes Care of Itself* by Bill Walsh (with Steve Jamison and Craig Walsh, 2010) and think about how the points raised therein relate to teaching. We will look at these further in Chapter 8. For more on independent learning and growth mindsets, have a look at *The Lazy Teacher's Handbook* by Jim Smith and Ian Gilbert (2010) and *Mindset* by Carol Dweck (2012).

For those who wish to go into more depth on independent learning, you can turn to:

- Pintrich, P.R., Meece, J.R. & Schunk, D.H. (2013) *Motivation in education: Theory, research, and applications.*
- Zimmerman, B.J. (2002). Becoming a self-regulated learner: an overview. *Theory into Practice*, 41(2), 64–72.

Habit Six: The Lens of Literacy

Two habits to go. The first of which requires us to turn our attention to literacy.

As with differentiation, literacy is a word which has lost some meaning and efficacy through its excessive use within educational discourse. This usage has been with good intentions, however, the extent of it has served to unhook the word from its moorings, causing it to float, somewhat capriciously, upon the sea of sense, being buffeted hither and thither by circumstance, convention and the user's intentions.

We will put an end to this.

Literacy means four things:

- Speaking
- Listening
- Reading
- Writing.

Cultivating the habits of outstanding teaching

It means nothing more and nothing less. Literacy is composed of our ability to listen and to speak as well as our ability to read and to write.

So, when we say that we must cultivate a habit called 'The Lens of Literacy', what we mean is that we must look at what we do in the classroom through the perspective of supporting and improving the speaking, listening, reading and writing of our students.

This is necessary whoever we are. It is not a habit restricted to teachers of English.

Every teacher is a teacher of literacy.

Frequently, we teach literacy skills and improve the speaking, listening, reading and writing abilities of our pupils without even realising it. This is an inevitable consequence of the fact that language is central to communication and that communication is central to teaching.

What is more, most of the curriculum is concerned with the four elements of literacy. Further, every part of the curriculum is at least closely connected to these elements.

This leads us on to a point which transcends the classroom.

Being able to speak, listen, read and write means being given access to the world in which we live, as well as to our own thoughts and ideas. It means having the means through which we can communicate with others, articulate that which is inside us and share this with the people with whom we come into contact. Literacy bridges the gaps between minds. It allows us to name and know the worlds we encounter – the external world, the internal world (of introspection) and the world of culture which springs up in between the first two (and which overlaps with both in many places).

On a human level, then, it is our duty as teachers to give attention to literacy, such that we might help our pupils to better communicate with themselves and with others.

On a pragmatic level, outstanding teaching and learning cannot happen if we do not give thought to literacy.

If we fail to take account of the speaking, listening, reading and writing that our students do – or that we ask them to do as part of our lessons – then we will be failing to attend to the most fundamental tools in which our students need to be proficient if they are to achieve highly and secure great progress.

It is for these reasons that every teacher is a teacher of literacy.

We might also say that it is for these reasons that every student is a student of literacy. Not in the sense that they will necessarily study it as a discrete subject (though, of course, they will do at various points in primary and secondary school), but in the sense that their entire school career is in large part a history of the development of their ability to read, write, speak and listen with skill, care, precision and accuracy.

In terms of the habit then, we need to be thinking about the four elements of literacy when we are planning, teaching, interacting and marking. Doing this will help us to examine what we can do throughout our time as teachers to facilitate the development of our students' literacy skills.

This will have two benefits. First, it will have the absolute benefit of improving the abilities of our pupils. Second, it will have the instrumental benefit of giving them greater means through which to engage with the learning we want them to do. This, in turn, will lead to them making better progress – and more sustained progress – than if we did not pay attention to literacy or include it as one of our habits.

For more on literacy in general terms, pick up any general undergraduate psychology textbook. Most, if not all, of these contain sections on language development. For a more specific insight, look at undergraduate textbooks focused specifically on developmental or cognitive psychology. You might also like to take a look at *Don't Call it Literacy!* by Geoff Barton (2012) and the wonderful *Orality and Literacy* by Walter Ong (2012). Finally, for a wider insight into language, try *How Language Works* by David Crystal (2007).

Habit Seven: Creating Clarity and Confusion

Our final habit focuses on how we communicate in the classroom.

Specifically, it looks at how we explain things and how we ask questions.

Both of these jobs are central to what teachers do on a daily basis.

We begin from a position of greater knowledge and understanding than our pupils. This acts as a starting point from which we can help students to make progress. As part of our work, we seek to shed light on ideas and information, so pupils can come to understand them. In addition, we use questioning to stretch and challenge the thinking that students do.

And this is where our title comes in.

Outstanding teaching relies on our ability both to create clarity, through careful and thoughtfully conceived explanations, and to sow confusion, through thought-provoking and challenging questions.

Let us attend to each of these in turn, so that we might further emphasise their importance.

First, we will look at explaining.

There are many ways in which we can explain information and ideas to our students. A large number of these are outlined in Chapter 10. What we need to think about here, though, is what explanation means in practice, why it is essential to outstanding teaching and how we can ensure our explanations are of the highest standard.

To begin, we can note that explaining is something we do on a regular basis, throughout our teaching. We explain things verbally and in writing. We explain to the whole class, to groups and to individuals.

Our explanations concern the content of our lessons as well as procedural matters such as how to complete tasks. They also cover supplementary areas such as classroom rules, behaviour management and pastoral matters.

Whenever we are explaining, our purpose is to help students understand what it is at issue – whether that is something they need to know or something they need to do.

In this sense, our explanations are instructional, as well as elucidatory. The purpose, in practice, is to provide pupils with access to certain things. And, often, for them to then do things as a result.

We can therefore see why excellent explanations are an integral part of outstanding teaching.

If we don't explain things well, we diminish the chance that students will be successful. Further, we limit the amount of progress they can make. Finally, we run the risk of inefficiency. Poor explanations lead to the need for additional explanations; they may also provoke uncertainty and disengagement.

To ensure our explanations regularly reach the highest standards, we need to do three simple things.

First, we need to pay attention to the language we use. This involves thinking in advance about how to phrase our speech and writing – even rehearsing it on occasion if that seems necessary.

Second, we need to gauge how students respond to the explanations we give. We can then use this information to modify and adapt what we do next.

Third, we should make use of a variety of explanatory techniques, as outlined in Chapter 10.

We move now to the second part of the seventh habit – creating confusion.

This concerns questioning.

Outstanding teaching sees teachers using their questioning to consistently push the thinking of their students. In doing this, we help pupils to make more progress, to think more deeply and to take their learning to places they probably would not have accessed on their own.

Effective questioning comes in many forms. Common to all examples, however, are the following points:

Cultivating the habits of outstanding teaching

- The questioning is closely tied to where students are at in terms of their learning.

- The questioning pushes pupils to develop their thinking (this could be in all manner of different ways).

- The questioning is delivered skilfully – the teacher responds to what they hear, gives thinking time, presses students to explain themselves more clearly and isn't afraid to adopt different roles in order to facilitate greater progress.

You will note that outstanding questioning is predicated on the teacher tailoring the questions they ask. It also sees the teacher setting out with the express aim of helping students to think differently, and more deeply, about the topic at issue.

This is the kind of questioning we all want to achieve in our classrooms, and it is the kind of questioning which, allied to effective explanations and the cultivation of habits 1–6, will result in students making significant learning gains.

With that said, we draw our introductory analysis of the seven habits of outstanding teaching to a close.

The final thing to note before we move on is that habits need to be cultivated – we need to embed them in what we do by regularly repeating relevant processes and ways of acting. Knowing why each of the habits is important can help us to appreciate the significance of this throughout our often hectic and demanding working lives.

3 Cultivating the habits of outstanding learning

Having considered the habits of outstanding teaching, we will now look at the habits of outstanding learning. The aim here is to illustrate the ways of thinking and acting we want our students to develop if they are going to be successful.

Our purpose is twofold. First, we want to delineate the habits of mind which lead to outstanding learning. In doing this, we will provide a model which can be applied in any classroom. These habits are the ideal. They are the things we want all learners to strive towards. They are the things we can seek to cultivate in our classrooms every day.

Second, we want to illustrate the fact – central in everything we have said so far – that outstanding teaching is concerned primarily with learning. That is, to reiterate an earlier point, outstanding teaching is less about performance and the teacher than it is about learning and the students (with the former being facilitated by the teacher and the latter being supported by them).

As you read through the habits outlined below, what you will also notice is that they mesh with the habits outlined in the last chapter, as well as the principles enumerated in the introduction. This is necessary and important.

It is necessary because, if there was to be a disconnection between these three separate elements of outstanding teaching, then we would risk a situation in which our general arguments and specific recommendations lacked coherence and consistency. Such a lack would seriously undermine the quality of the argument at the same time as diminish the credibility of what we are suggesting.

It is important because, if we are to secure outstanding teaching in our classrooms on a regular basis, then we need to be confident that there is clarity of thought running through all that we do. The key benefit of this is that the decisions, judgements and assessments we make are made in relation to the same set of criteria, the same underlying intentions and the same guiding purposes.

If this was not the case, then we would find ourselves in a much weaker position. We would be harder pressed to ensure consistently outstanding teaching and we would struggle to join together the different parts of our practice – not least the learning that students do and the teaching we deliver in order to lead and facilitate that.

In conclusion, outstanding learning is intimately tied up with outstanding teaching. We need to be aware of the habits and principles which inform both if we are to be successful in our endeavours to raise achievement, secure progress and engage learners.

In the rest of this chapter we will examine the five habits of outstanding learning in order to do this.

Those five habits are:

- Habit One: High Expectations
- Habit Two: Expecting and Using Feedback
- Habit Three: Active Learning
- Habit Four: Embracing Mistakes
- Habit Five: Reflection.

We will look at each one in turn, offering an explanation and then connecting it to what we have already thought about in Chapters 1 and 2. Through this process, we will also signpost which of Chapters 4–10 will offer practical strategies linked to the habit in question.

Habit One: High Expectations

In John Hattie's book *Visible Learning* (2008), the author demonstrates that student perceptions and predictions of their own achievement are closely connected to the results those students achieve.

Pupils who perceive themselves as being unacademic, unable to learn or unlikely to make good progress are likely to live up to these labels. The same is true for students who view themselves in the opposite light.

We might sum this up in the following phrase:

Assumptions are the limits of our world.

It makes sense on a basic level. If we assume something about ourselves, then that assumption comes to play a part in our thinking. As a result, what we believe we can and can't do is, to some extent, dependent on the assumption.

If the assumption is negative or limiting, then it circumscribes our thinking. This, in turn, leads to circumscription of our behaviour. After all, the things we do and the actions we choose to take are, invariably, a direct result of our thinking – whether that thinking is conscious or subconscious.

We can use the example of two imaginary students to illustrate this point.

Student A believes they are a failure at school. They think that learning is not for them and that, no matter what they do, they will not be able to make any progress. As a result, they do not tend to put much effort in during lessons. What is more, they seek to protect their sense of self by disengaging from learning. They even look to develop conflict so as to provide an excuse for their lack of engagement as well as a means through which to gain status.

Student B believes they can succeed at school by working hard and targeting their effort on the things that matter. They see their own abilities as open to change and growth. They do not believe that intelligence is fixed. As a result, they engage positively with the learning presented to them in lessons. They enjoy trying new things and having their thinking challenged. They feel safe and secure at school, viewing teachers, lessons and the building itself from a positive perspective.

Clearly, it is much more likely that Student B will be successful. They will be much closer to the model of an outstanding learner than Student A. This is because they will be operating under a set of assumptions about learning, school and themselves which give rise to positive, proactive and open behaviour.

Student A is not at fault here. We are not making a value judgement about the two pupils. For whatever reason, they have developed the assumptions they currently possess.

What we are doing, though, is identifying the central importance of assumptions to learning and achievement. In addition, we are pointing to the fact that, as teachers, we want to be cultivating in all our pupils the habits of thought exhibited by Student B.

The best way in which to encapsulate all this is in the title of habit one: High Expectations.

A student who has high expectations of themselves and their learning is much more likely to hit high standards than a student who has low expectations or no expectations at all.

Of course, we want to avoid the situation developing wherein pupils have expectations so high that they foster anxiety.

That is why it is best to cultivate high expectations focused on effort and the exercise of one's own volition. This manifests itself in assumptions such as:

- If I work hard then I have a good chance of being successful.

- My own efforts are directly connected to my own success.

- I can change things by targeting my effort and working hard.

As you can see, these assumptions focus on processes rather than products. This helps to maintain high expectations without these expectations falling prey to the frustration which can arise from perfectionism unfulfilled (such as when we assume that we must make a piece of work perfect otherwise it will not be good enough).

Perfectionism can have a potentially deleterious effect as it brings with it the risk of myopia. In pursuit of perfection we lose sight of what we are trying to achieve (great learning) and why (to progress and to grow).

This is much less likely to happen if our high expectations are trained on effort and the exercise of our own agency.

To sum up what we have said so far:

- Student perceptions and assumptions play a big role in pupil achievement.
- Students who have high expectations of themselves and their learning are more likely to achieve well and view learning positively.
- Expectations should focus on processes rather than products because everyone can put effort in and everyone can continue to do this in order to learn and to grow.

We can connect this habit of outstanding learning to habits one, two, three and five of outstanding teaching:

- Habit One: Eliciting and Using Information should include us eliciting and using information about our students' self-perceptions and expectations of what they can do and achieve.
- Habit Two: Facilitating Progress sees us showing students that everyone can grow and achieve. It also allows us to provide feedback which builds up and supports high expectations.
- Habit Three: Personalising Learning includes us finding ways to ensure every student can experience success. This helps to build positive attitudes to learning and higher expectations of one's own potential.
- Habit Five: Leading Learning sees us communicating to pupils the fact that everybody has the potential to learn and to grow. It also includes us shaping and changing students' mindsets so that they are positive about learning.

The consequence of this is that many of the practical strategies, activities and techniques presented in Chapters 4, 5, 6 and 8 will help you to engender high expectations at the same time as they help you to secure the habits of outstanding teaching outlined in each section.

This once again illustrates the wider point about the symbiotic relationship between outstanding teaching and outstanding learning.

Habit Two: Expecting and Using Feedback

We noted earlier that feedback is the information students need in order to make great progress. This is where the teacher takes their superior knowledge and understanding and uses it to help show pupils where they should go next, where they need to target their effort and why this is the right thing to do.

We contrasted formative and summative feedback, demonstrating how the latter sums up learning and is therefore most useful for administrative purposes (including tracking and monitoring) and at the end of a course, whereas the former provides quality information students can use to secure progress, therefore making it most useful for facilitating and sustaining learning.

All this means that outstanding teaching should include regular formative feedback from the teacher. This can be verbal, written and, less often, non-verbal. All this links to habits one and two of outstanding teaching, as well as, less explicitly, habits three and five.

Given as how outstanding teaching will involve the regular use of formative feedback, it follows that outstanding learning should encompass the expectation that such feedback will be forthcoming, as well as the understanding that this feedback needs to be effectively implemented if great progress is to be made.

We will split this point up and deal with each section in turn.

Students who expect summative feedback for their work are operating under the assumption that this feedback will help them to learn and progress. However, this is a false assumption.

A grade, mark or level does not provide pupils with any insight into why they have achieved that result or what they need to do to improve.

Therefore, any perceived learning benefit is really only a knock-on effect of the psychological impact caused by receiving the grade, level or mark.

For example, a student who is expecting a C and gets a D may say to themselves: 'I must work harder.' This consequence is not a function of the grade itself. Nothing in the letter 'D' says that the pupil must work harder. Instead, it is a consequence of the student's thinking in relation to that grade. In this case, that thinking centres on a sense that expectations have not been met and therefore something must be done.

The problem is that, even in a best-case scenario such as this, where the summative grade ends up pushing pupils to further apply themselves, no guidance is given as to how they should work harder or why.

It may be the case that the pupils apply themselves in the wrong direction. Maybe they will focus on material of which they actually demonstrated a good understanding. Or, perhaps, and more seriously, it may be the case that the area in which they have lost marks is one they cannot improve without clear guidance from the teacher (as in the case of exam technique).

All this further reinforces the point that only formative feedback *guarantees* that information is passing from teacher to student, concerning assessment, which is centred on learning and what needs to be done for pupils to make progress.

If students get into the habit of expecting formative feedback on a regular basis, good things will result. These include:

- Pupils will come to understand why formative feedback is better and how this type of feedback leads to learning gains.

- The teacher will be reminded (in case they forget) that provision of formative feedback is one of the habits of outstanding teaching.

43

Cultivating the habits of outstanding learning

- Students will continually know what their targets are in terms of learning. They will then be in a position to continually work towards these targets so as to make progress and be successful.

This last point takes us to the second part of habit two – using feedback.

It is all very well pupils coming to expect formative feedback but if we want this feedback to translate into significant learning gains, they must also become habituated to the idea of regularly implementing this feedback.

If students do not implement the feedback they are given, then they will not make outstanding progress.

One of the simplest things the teacher can do in order to cultivate this habit in their students is to set aside lesson time during which the focus is on implementing feedback. This could be at the start of lessons, at the start of activities or even in the form of a plenary.

The form is not hugely important. What is important is that it happens some way or another and that students get used to this.

Repetition, allied to explicit discussion of why it is necessary and appropriate, will go a long way towards habituating pupils into this way of thinking.

Over time, one wants to be in a position where students are actively seeking formative feedback so that they might put it into practice immediately and, as a result, make great learning gains lesson after lesson.

To get a sense of what this will look like, imagine someone learning to drive who has a strong desire to pass their test relatively quickly. Such a person would seek formative feedback from their instructor at every opportunity and would then try to implement this feedback wherever possible so as to become a better driver.

Habit two is all about fostering such an attitude in our students' minds in relation to the learning which goes on in our class-rooms.

As we noted earlier, this habit links to habits one, two, three and five of outstanding teaching. In the case of the first two, that is because both of those are concerned with what the teacher can do to assess pupils' learning and then facilitate progress.

In the case of habit three, it is because part of personalising learning is the delivery of personalised feedback. And, in terms of habit five, it is because leading learning will always involve the promotion of good habits of mind to the students you teach, including the expectation that formative feedback will be provided and that this should be implemented wherever possible.

Habit Three: Active Learning

By active learning we do not mean students getting up and moving around. That can form part of active learning but it is not active learning per se.

By active learning we mean that students are paying active attention to that about which they are learning. This means that pupils are actively engaging with ideas and information. In so doing, they will be taking control of their minds and directing their efforts towards the task in hand. This will allow them to learn more. It will also mean that their learning is of a higher quality.

Let me illustrate this so as to reinforce the point.

Consider the difference between passive reading and active reading.

When we read passively we do not attend closely to the words on the page. While we read them we may think of other things or we may allow them to wash over us in something of a fug.

Passive reading takes on different forms and runs to different degrees. For example, we might read a newspaper passively while waiting for a train. Or, we might read a light novel before going to bed. In the latter case, we may be paying some attention but it is likely that, overall, our minds will remain fairly passive.

When we read actively, we pay close attention to the words on the page. We think about them, what they mean and how they connect to other things we know and have experienced.

Cultivating the habits of outstanding learning

Active reading forges new connections in our brains, causes us to remember and learn from the text in question, and engages our mind in the process. Consider reading you did at university. Much of this will have been active. You will have been reading with the intention of trying to understand. This intention will have animated your efforts, leading you to read actively.

Another example is the experience we have when we are deeply engaged with a novel. Hours can pass during which our attention is completely wrapped up in the fictional world the author has created. Here, again, we find our mind actively engaged – we are thinking about the words, imagining the places, people and events which have been described and so forth.

These two examples neatly illustrate the difference between active and passive learning.

The former involves engagement and agency. The latter does not.

Clearly, we will learn more if we are thinking actively.

In terms of the classroom, active learning is synonymous with active thinking. It can involve all manner of different tasks or cognitive processes, including:

- speaking
- listening
- reading
- writing
- interacting
- problem-solving
- thinking
- failing
- trying again
- reflecting
- analysing

- judging
- creating
- questioning
- remembering
- assessing
- investigating.

In each case, the point is simply that the student is actively engaged with what is going on. It is for this reason that good-quality tasks, lesson planning and questioning are so important to outstanding teaching. These are the things which help to stimulate pupils' minds and create the kind of active thinking we want them to do on a regular basis.

Active learning as a habit of outstanding learning means having students who understand:

- The importance of actively engaging with tasks, information and ideas.
- The difference between passive learning and active learning.
- The fact that active learning does not necessarily mean getting up and moving round (but is actually to do with what is happening in your mind as well as the ways in which you choose to use your mind).

As has been noted, we can promote and encourage this understanding through the use of high-quality tasks and questioning, as well as through the development of thoughtful and engaging lessons.

In addition, we can seek to cultivate the habit by talking to our students, helping them to reflect and demonstrating for them the different results which stem from passive and active thinking.

In terms of talking to pupils, we can do this throughout lessons. It can involve speaking to groups, to the whole class or to students one on one.

Cultivating the habits of outstanding learning

Whichever method you choose to take, the aim will be the same: to use the language of active learning as a model which students can internalise. They will then be able to use the language in their own speech and as part of their own thinking.

For example, we might ask a group of students how they are thinking about a particular task. We could then pick up on any active processes they mention and use these as a starting point to briefly discuss why this type of thinking is beneficial.

Regarding helping pupils to reflect, we can use mid-lesson reviews, plenaries and reflective discussion activities to encourage students to think about the type of thinking they are doing and to analyse and evaluate the efficacy of this.

I am sure that you will see the connection here to ideas surrounding metacognition. Or, to apply its other name, thinking about thinking.

In a sense, this habit is about two things which exist in tandem with one another. The first is the active thinking, and by extension active learning, which students do. The second is the awareness they develop about this thinking.

The former without the latter will not be as effective. This is because students will not be in a position to learn about the effects of their own thinking. Therefore, they will not be as well placed to control and direct their own learning.

Finally, we as teachers can demonstrate to our students why active thinking and active learning are better than their passive counterparts. We can do this through modelling, by drawing attention to the results of different types of thinking and learning and through the feedback we provide to pupils.

This habit connects closely to all the habits of outstanding teaching outlined in Chapter 2; it is not possible to dismiss its connection to any single one. In short, active learning – paying attention to our thinking and directing that thinking effectively – links closely to all aspects of outstanding teaching.

Habit Four: Embracing Mistakes

Mistakes are brilliant!

Mistakes are how we learn. If we don't make mistakes – if we don't fail – then we struggle to make progress, to grow and to develop.

Unfortunately, many students are fearful of making mistakes and terrified of failure. Quite why this is so is open to question. A number of points suggest themselves, such as social pressure, parental expectations and wider notions of success and failure.

Whatever leads pupils to fear mistakes, we need to overcome this attitude and instead cultivate growth mindsets in relation to learning. This term stems from the work of the psychologist Carol Dweck who has done much research into success, learning and the way in which we perceive ourselves (as well as the impact this has on our actions and thoughts).

A mindset is the beliefs we hold about a certain aspect of ourselves. A fixed mindset assumes that change is impossible and that what we have is what there shall always be, for evermore. A growth mindset, however, assumes that change, progress and development can and do happen; that we are in control of ourselves; and that, through our own volition, we can make changes and grow.

A growth mindset in the context of learning will always be more conducive to securing progress and raising achievement.

Three important features of growth mindsets connect to this idea of making mistakes. They are:

- A desire to seek out challenges and to use these as opportunities for learning.
- A perception that mistakes present information which can be used for learning.
- A belief that growth and change are a result of targeted effort and that, therefore, mistakes are neither damaging nor a threat.

The corollary of this is that we can stimulate growth mindset thinking by focusing on the issue of embracing mistakes.

Cultivating the habits of outstanding learning

Establishing a classroom environment in which mistakes are celebrated, used and encouraged will help your students to quickly develop the habit of seeing mistakes positively. This will have the knock-on effect of encouraging growth mindsets across the board.

At this point, it will be useful for us to look in greater depth at the reasoning underpinning our argument about mistakes.

Success teaches us little. It rarely gives us information we can use to improve. Sometimes, when we are successful, we can analyse what we have done and the results which stemmed from this in order to ascertain why we were successful.

Frequently, however, success brings with it little or no information we can use.

However, mistakes, by their very nature, always present us with information we can use to grow, to learn and to develop. Whenever we make a mistake we find ourselves in a position to analyse and evaluate why we weren't successful. In many cases, the consequences of the mistake itself are sufficient to illustrate the why to us.

This points to the fact that mistakes and failure automatically generate information we can use for the purposes of learning, whereas success does no such thing.

Of course, it goes without saying that, ultimately, it is success each of us is seeking – both for ourselves and for our students. But it is learning from mistakes which helps us to grow and, by extension, achieve the success we desire more quickly.

In the classroom, mistakes present teacher and student with the chance to move the learning on. They are a fulcrum about which the hands of progress can turn.

Every pupil makes mistakes in lessons; most students make mistakes every lesson, every day. These mistakes might be big or they might be small. They could be influential or they could be barely noticeable.

What remains true throughout, though, is the fact that every student has before them, day-after-day, information which they could use, potentially, to learn, and to learn quickly and effectively.

If you can get your pupils to embrace mistakes and to see the benefits they bring (alongside the fact that fearing mistakes and failure is not only pointless but also a serious waste of time and energy), then you will have a group of students who take advantage of every learning opportunity that comes their way during your lessons.

So, for example, your pupils will be using the opportunities mistakes present to reflect on what they have done and the reasons why things did not pan out as expected.

Over time, this will create a virtuous cycle in which students are continually learning and growing as a direct result of their own efforts (and the failures and mistakes which these bring).

One of the best ways in which to cultivate this habit is to celebrate mistakes. As part of this, you can also share your own experiences of mistakes. In both cases, you should illustrate to pupils why it is that the mistakes are or were good. This can be done by showing quite clearly what benefits the mistakes lead to in terms of learning.

The habit of embracing mistakes connects to habits two, five, six and seven of outstanding teaching.

Habit Two, Facilitating Progress, is obvious: embracing mistakes has a big part to play in securing great progress.

Habit Five, Leading Learning, is also straightforward. As part of leading the learning in your classroom, you will need to prioritise the positive reconceptualisation of mistakes and failure. It will be up to you to create a safe, affirming atmosphere in which mistakes are openly encouraged and in which they are seen as a vital learning opportunity.

Habit Six, The Lens of Literacy, connects to embracing mistakes in the sense that reading, writing, speaking and listening are the foundations of learning. Therefore, if we are to continually secure great progress across the board, we should encourage students to embrace mistakes in the context of these four core skills. This will help us to raise literacy levels throughout our classes.

Finally, Habit Seven, Creating Clarity and Confusion, connects to embracing mistakes in terms of its second half – confusion. Pushing students' thinking and helping them to perceive their ideas in a more nuanced light will be more effective if those students are primed to see mistakes as a good thing. This will mean they do not hold on to their existing beliefs as strongly and remain more open and positive to having their thinking challenged.

Habit Five: Reflection

Reflection is the means through which we look back at what we have done so that we might analyse it, assess it and, as a result of these two processes, learn from it.

Those who do not reflect tend not to learn from their mistakes. What is more, they tend to lack insight when it comes to their own learning and the thought processes which they use in the classroom.

As you will no doubt know from experience, pupils who have an inclination towards reflection often make excellent progress. They are able to take control of their learning, doing so by examining what they have done and assessing whether it worked or not.

Through the quality of their work these pupils illustrate the benefits of reflection. They are able to produce material which is superior to that of their peers (in terms of progress) because they can use knowledge of their own thinking and learning to grow the quality of what they do.

Pupils who do not think about their thinking and learning miss out on the opportunity to continually learn about what they have done. They also miss out on the chance to continually refine their work. In so doing, they put themselves (unintentionally, of course) at a considerable disadvantage.

As with the other habits of outstanding learning, the central issue here is that it is better to do the habit than not because this doing unlocks learning that would have otherwise been missed or inaccessible.

When it comes to reflection, we must be careful to note that what we are really talking about is critical reflection.

Reflection means simply to look at that which we have done. This, on its own, is unlikely to bring benefits.

Critical reflection means to look at that which we have done through a critical lens. That lens is made up of analysis and evaluation – the two underlying constituents of critical thinking. By looking at what we have done from an analytical and an evaluative perspective, we find ourselves able to elicit information which we can use to help us to learn and progress.

Taking analysis first, we can note that this process involves breaking down that which we are looking at into its component parts. As part of this process, we examine the connections, purposes and structures of these parts. This helps us to understand them better.

Moving on to evaluation, we can see that the information we draw out through the process of analysis comes to inform any assessments we make. It does this by giving us an insight into the make-up and nature of the thing in question. Having this knowledge places us in a stronger position to make a sound judgement – seeing as how we have more information to go on than would otherwise be the case.

Drawing this general discussion back to critical reflection in the classroom, we can say that the process allows us to:

- Analyse the thinking and learning we have done.

- Consider the results of this thinking and learning, including the successes and failures.

- Compare what we did with what we intended to do or what we had hoped to do.

- Make a judgement about the relative effectiveness of the different parts of our thinking and learning.

- Make a judgement about the effectiveness of our thinking and learning as a whole.

Cultivating the habits of outstanding learning

The process of critical reflection thus allows us to harness the power of analysis and evaluation in order to improve and develop our learning and our thinking.

This is a process of which you will have first-hand experience.

All teachers engage in critical reflection. Some do it in the first few years of their practice; some continue to do it throughout their career.

This reflection usually takes the form of sitting down after a lesson (directly after or later on in the day) and thinking about what worked and what didn't, why this was the case and what the prospects are for improving matters.

As teachers, we are thus in a position to fully understand the benefits that can be derived from regular reflection.

If we can get our students to regularly reflect on what they are doing in lessons – both in terms of their thinking and in terms of their learning – then we will be helping them to make much better progress than would otherwise be the case.

There are many ways in which we can promote the use of critical reflection in the classroom. The most obvious are:

- Plenaries
- Reviews
- Questioning which stimulates or encourages reflective thinking
- Learning diaries
- Reflective discussion activities (in groups, in pairs or as a whole class).

In each case, the purpose is to provide a structure through which pupils can critically reflect. Simply leaving it up to students to reflect on their own is not enough; what is to say that they will do it? And, as importantly, what is to say that they will possess the requisite skills to do it well?

Critical reflection needs to be taught, just like all other skills, if it is to be done consistently well across the board.

At this point, we can turn back to the habits of outstanding teaching in order to connect these to our fifth and final habit of outstanding learning.

As with habit three, reflection connects closely to all the habits of outstanding teaching. In terms of habits one and two, we want to be using the information we elicit to help students to reflect, just as we want to be promoting critical reflection through the targets we set and the lessons we plan.

Habit Three, Personalising Learning, includes personalisation of reflection.

Habit Four, Building Expertise, includes the promotion of student reflection under three of its subcategories: expertise in pedagogy, expertise in psychology and expertise regarding the students you teach.

Habit Five, Leading Learning, connects to reflection in the sense that you will be leading your students in thinking reflectively and that you will be showing them how they can go about doing this.

Habit Six, The Lens of Literacy, involves reflection in as much as pupils will develop their reading, writing, speaking and listening skills more quickly and more effectively if they can critically reflect on these as they go.

And, finally, Habit Seven, Creating Clarity and Confusion, links to reflection in the sense that we want students to reflect back on why particular explanations lead to clarity and why certain questions and ideas cause the confusion or challenge that they do.

There we have it.

The five habits of outstanding learning:

- High Expectations
- Expecting and Using Feedback
- Active Learning
- Embracing Mistakes
- Reflection.

Cultivating the habits of outstanding learning

Each one closely connected to the seven habits of outstanding teaching. All of them connected together and most effective if they can be cultivated alongside one another.

In the chapters which follow, we will look at practical measures through which you can implement the seven habits of outstanding teaching. These measures will also help you to cultivate and develop the five habits of outstanding learning.

The two go hand in hand, as we have seen and as we shall continue to see through the remainder of this book.

4 Assessment in the round

Habit One: Eliciting and Using Information

Assessment is one of the three key features of teaching, along with planning and teaching lessons. While there are many more things to the job, these three categories cover the basics of what we do.

We plan our lessons. Then we teach them. Then we assess what students have done.

Except, we don't!

Not if we want to be outstanding.

Instead, we see assessment as something which runs through our planning and our teaching, as well as being something which comes afterwards.

So, for example, not only does assessment encompass marking students' books but it also entails eliciting and using information through the course of a lesson, providing feedback while pupils are working, opening up success criteria and planning and preparing appropriate assessments and assessment opportunities.

This is what we mean by assessment in the round: building assessment into everything we do. We will explore this topic, along with habit one, in practical terms by breaking it down into five separate categories. We will follow this same structure in the subsequent chapters as well.

Planning and preparing assessments and assessment opportunities

We have noted that eliciting and using information is central to outstanding teaching. It is this which allows us to create a positive feedback loop through which we can continually match our teaching to the needs of our pupils. In addition, this also allows us to give effective, relevant and targeted formative feedback to our students. When done consistently, both of these lead to outstanding progress.

We will look at methods through which to elicit information below. Here, we will think about ways in which we can plan and prepare so as to create situations from which we can elicit information.

To begin with, we need to alter how we think about lesson planning.

We must start to take account of two things:

1. What kind of information the tasks and activities we use will allow us to elicit.

2. What kind of information formal assessments will allow us to elicit and how we will be able to use that information in the context of the scheme of work.

In the first case, this involves us thinking about the assessment opportunities our tasks and activities will bring. This might lead us to choose different tasks and activities from those we normally use, so as to ensure we can elicit a greater amount of information.

In the second case, this involves thinking about the timing of formal assessments and the types of questions or tasks we will include in these.

When it comes to the tasks and activities we use in lessons, some are better for eliciting information than others. In addition, different types of task yield different types of information. For example, a writing task presents us with information in the form of written work whereas a discussion task presents us with information in the form of speech.

Here are some practical suggestions on the types of tasks you can use at different points of the lesson in order to elicit rich and useful information:

Starters. At the beginning of the lesson we are often looking for information which gives us an insight into what students remember from the previous lesson or what they already know about the topic of study.

We can use starter activities such as:

- List all the things you know about the topic.

- What three things do you know about the topic and what would you like to find out?

- Interview three other people in the class to find out what they know about the topic and be ready to share this at the end of the activity.

- How would you answer this question about last lesson's learning?

- How might this image connect to the lesson title?

You will notice that, in each case, the starter is focused on getting pupils thinking and learning at the same time as it aims to elicit information that will be of use to the teacher.

Activities. During the main section of lessons, we want to be able to elicit information about how students are learning and how they are interacting with the lesson content. The following task types are some of those which are open to us:

- Discussion activities. These allow us to listen to what students are thinking. This gives us an insight into how they are engaging with the learning.

- Written activities. These allow us to walk around the room and read what pupils are writing. This gives us a window into their thoughts and ideas.

- Group work activities. These usually contain a range of elements including discussion and writing, all of which are underpinned by the interactions between group members. Here we can elicit information through listening and reading as well as through observation.

The list could go on to cover many more task types (and later on we will look at some specific examples).

The point, though, is to demonstrate how information can be elicited from these different tasks. This, in turn, helps us to start looking at planning through the lens of assessment. Thus, we can always ask ourselves the question: Have I planned at least one activity through which I will be able to elicit the information I want about students' learning?

Plenaries. At the end of the lesson, we want to elicit information about what pupils have learnt overall. We tend to be particularly concerned with their understanding of the key learning points we identified in our outcomes and objectives.

All plenaries elicit information about prior learning. They cannot help but do this given their structure. Therefore, making time for plenaries and including them as a standard part of your planning will help you to regularly elicit information at the end of lessons which you can use to adapt and change what you plan to do next time.

We move now to think about formal assessments. Two points are worth noting here.

First, you should think carefully about what information any formal assessment is likely to elicit. For example, it might be that you want to know how your pupils are faring in relation to a particular theme which runs through the subject you are teaching (such as interpretation in History teaching).

Thinking about this in advance will allow you to structure your formal assessment in such a way as to elicit the information you want. Failing to think like this means you might get the information you want, or you might not.

As ever, it is better to plan ahead, harness your skills and ensure you get the results you are after, rather than hit and hope.

Second, we should give attention to the timing of formal assessments.

We have noted that the necessary supplement to eliciting information is using that information. If we consistently plan formal assessments for the end of units of work, this makes it harder for us to use the information we elicit in a really effective manner.

A better approach might be to plan assessments for mid-way through a unit of work so that we can use the information we elicit while we are still teaching the topic, therefore adapting what we do to fit with the knowledge and understanding our pupils have developed.

However, if we have to have our assessments at the end of a unit of work, for whatever reason, we might decide to plan them so that we elicit information about skills, which we can then use to adapt what we do, regardless of the topic we are teaching.

Assessment for learning

Underlying everything we are saying here about assessment is the research into assessment for learning we flagged up in Chapter 2.

We noted that assessment for learning involves three things:

- Eliciting and using information
- Providing formative feedback
- Opening up success criteria.

We will look at each of these in practical terms shortly. Before we do, we need to attend to the phrase 'assessment for learning' so that we can help ourselves to think about assessment and Habit One: Eliciting and Using Information in a sustainable fashion.

Assessment for learning sits in contrast to assessment of learning. The latter is about summing up what has been learnt and assigning a grade, mark or level. The former is about using assessment for the purposes of learning: to facilitate progress.

Using assessment for the purposes of learning is great. As we have been saying, it is one of the hallmarks of outstanding teaching. What we need to be careful of is the risk that our knowledge and understanding of this fact does not wane or fade over time. I mention this because it is very easy for this exact thing to happen.

Nearly all of us have been through an education system in which summative assessment is king. What is more, we live in a society in which summative assessment is frequently held up as an exemplar or as the arbiter of quality – be that on a CV, in league tables or in a report in a national newspaper.

This fact means that, to some extent, we will always be rowing against the tide when it comes to advocating and teaching according to the principles of assessment for learning.

This can throw up a number of problems and it would be remiss of me not to address these here. They are, after all, practical in nature, and this section of the book is concerned with matters practical.

The first issue we need to think about is the expectations and desires of your students.

It is highly likely that your pupils will have a set view of assessment and that view will be predicated on the notion that summative assessment is what assessment is, was and will forever be. The consequence of this fact is that pupils may react negatively to your attempts to introduce the aspects of assessment for learning into your teaching.

It is unlikely that they will be particularly perturbed by your attempts to elicit information through tasks and activities. However, they may well respond poorly (at least at first) to the provision of formative comments rather than summative grades, the use of whole-class feedback techniques (see below) and the scheduling of assessments during, rather than at the end of, units of work.

The best way I have found to overcome any resistance is a two-pronged approach.

In the first place, it is advisable to talk to your students about what assessment for learning is, why it works, how it works and what it means in the context of Habit One: Eliciting and Using Information.

There is a strong logic underpinning everything we are talking about in this chapter and this, alongside the research supporting the approach's efficacy, is hard for students to argue with. Also, talking pupils through the reasons behind your decisions will model excellent thinking for them; this is an added benefit we can derive from dealing with the problem in this way.

In the second place, take advantage of the fact that pupils quickly get habituated to ways of doing things. While they may react badly at first – perhaps kicking up a fuss or responding poorly to your innovations – it is highly likely that these reactions will fade away over a fairly short space of time.

There are a few reasons for this. First, school is an institution with a rigid structure. It does not take long, within this context, for changes to become normalised. Second, young people can often react to change without first thinking about it. The reaction is as much about signalling surprise or shock as it is about genuine preference for the previous way of doing things. Third, a lot happens at school every day. This means negative feelings towards changes and innovations in the classroom are quickly washed away and forgotten about.

The second issue we need to think about is colleagues.

If the people you work with are not used to thinking about assessment in the way we are here advocating, they may question your judgement or the professional choices you are making.

Rather than see this as a bad thing, embrace it.

Should this happen to you it represents a perfect opportunity to explain to your colleagues the evidence and reasoning which together illustrate why assessment for learning, and all which that entails, is such a good strategy to use in the classroom.

Furthermore, you can talk to them about the habits of out-standing teaching, indicating what these are and what role eliciting and using information plays. You might even tell them about this book!

The final issue to consider is parents.

One of the things we soon realise as a teacher is that everybody went to school and everybody's view of education tends to be shaped by their own experiences of schooling. This is completely natural. It is to be expected. We were no doubt the same when we first entered the profession (and perhaps still find our thinking influenced by our own school career).

However, it may be the case that a parent encountering your assessment methods, either directly or through what their children tell them, questions what you are doing. Again, it is best to embrace this rather than become defensive.

Should such a situation occur, remember once again that you are in a strong position to explain clearly why it is that this approach to assessment is so beneficial to the pupils you teach – in terms of securing progress and raising achievement.

Before we move on to look at practical strategies connected to each of the three aspects of assessment for learning, let me just make three final points.

First, nowhere here are we suggesting you shouldn't engage in summative assessment. You should. And then you should record the grades in your mark book and give formative feedback to your pupils.

Second, nowhere are we suggesting that you shouldn't tell students their grades. What we are saying is that the emphasis should be on formative feedback and grades only need to be shared at certain times of the year.

Third, eliciting and using information is the habit; assessment for learning is the approach which underpins the habit. The two are connected but not identical. The one is the basis of the other.

Eliciting and using information

We move now to think about some of the practical strategies you can employ in order to elicit information about your students' learning. Once you have elicited this information, you can then use it to adapt and develop your teaching.

Here we will outline eleven strategies suitable for use in any classroom.

1 Whole-class feedback techniques

Whole-class feedback (WCF) techniques are means through which you can elicit information from everyone in your class at the same time. They are a great way to check learning mid-lesson. You can use the information you receive to judge whether you should move on or revisit what you have just done.

Three WCF techniques are:

1. Thumbs. Ask students to show you their thumbs. 'Thumbs up' means they feel confident with the learning. 'Thumbs middle' means they feel OK but might need some more help. 'Thumbs down' means they are not OK and want to go over it again.

2. Mini-whiteboards. Hand out a class set of mini-whiteboards. Ask the class questions about the learning. They write their answers on their whiteboards and then show these to you.

3. Fingers. Present a question connected to the learning along with five possible answers. Ask students to hold up the number of fingers which represent what they think the answer is.

2 Discussion activities

Discussion activities give you the opportunity to listen to students. What they say will give you a big insight into what they are thinking about the learning. You can listen without responding, taking in the information for later use, or you can respond to it immediately by asking questions based on what you hear.

Discussion activities can involve pairs, groups or the whole class. Pairs and groups are the best for eliciting information as they involve everyone discussing at the same time. You can walk around the room and listen to the different conversations which are taking place.

3 Exit passes

Create a class set of strips of paper. There should be one per student. At the end of the lesson, display a question on the board and hand out the slips of paper. The question should refer to the learning which has taken place during the lesson. It could be in the form of a plenary or it could be a standalone question.

Ask pupils to write an answer to the question on their piece of paper and to hand this in on their way out. You can then look through the answers later on. They will give you an excellent insight into your class's thinking.

As an alternative, ask pupils to indicate on the piece of paper what they didn't understand. You can see from this suggestion that the technique can be adapted to elicit different kinds of information.

4 Plenaries

Plenaries require students to manipulate the learning they have done through the course of the lesson. The purpose is to help them to reinforce that knowledge and understanding in their own minds.

However, another benefit of plenaries it that, through them, you can elicit lots of information about the learning your pupils have done during the lesson. This could be written, spoken or in a visual form. Whatever approach you opt for, the result will be the same: you will end the lesson in possession of a large amount of rich, relevant information you can use to inform and adapt your future planning.

5 Questioning

We will look more at questioning in Chapter 10. Here, it is suffice to say that asking questions always elicits information from pupils.

The answers they give will provide you with an insight into what they have learnt and how they are thinking about the topic.

You might ask questions of individuals, groups or the whole class. In the first case, you will be able to tailor your questions so that they are highly relevant to the students in question and the existing knowledge you have about their learning and understanding.

6 Products

Products are those things that students produce in a lesson – essays, leaflets and role plays for example. Through reading, watching or listening to the products students produce, you will be able to easily elicit information about their thinking.

A good tip here is to set specific criteria which must be fulfilled in the creation of the product. This way, you can exert some control over the type of information you elicit. (This ties into our earlier point about planning opportunities for assessment.)

7 Self- and peer-assessment

We will look at these in more detail in the section below on opening up success criteria. Here, we can note that self- and peer-assessment exercises result in written or verbal information concerning what students think about their own work or learning or that of their peers.

This information provides two valuable insights. First, it gives us an assessment of the work or learning from the student's perspective. Second, it shows us how pupils are thinking about the topic and how they understand the nature of assessment in the subject. This information is gleaned through a brief analysis of how students have conducted their self- or peer-assessment, the kind of language they have used and the judgements they have made.

8 Marking

This is an obvious one. Marking pupils' work means gaining a sense of where they are at, what they are thinking and how they are learning.

You should mark regularly in order to elicit all this. When you do, record your summative assessments in your mark book. In addition, take the opportunity to provide formative feedback.

9 Listening

Listening is an underrated skill in the teacher's toolkit. We have already alluded to its efficacy in the earlier comments related to discussion.

It is good to remember that any time a student is talking in class, we are in a position to listen to them. By making sure our listening is active (i.e. by attending actively to what is being said), we can draw out all sorts of useful information about pupils' thoughts, views, misconceptions and learning.

10 Observing

Observing works in the same way as listening in the sense that it is a general method for eliciting information we can use throughout our time in the classroom.

For example, we can observe students while they are engaged in group work. If we see a pupil who looks to be struggling, we can go over to them and offer help and support.

Another helpful aspect of observing is that we can elicit information about students' moods, attitudes and feelings. Thus, if we sense that a pupil is upset, fed up or bored, we can use this information to inform how we interact with them, giving us the best chance possible of supporting them and helping them to get the most out of the lesson.

11 Circulating

Our final technique is circulating. This combines listening and observing. It involves walking round the classroom while pupils are working. Doing this gives us a great chance to see and hear what is going on.

All the time we are circulating we are using our senses to elicit information. We can then use this information to inform our actions. So, for example, if we observe a student near the back of the class struggling to get down to work, we can go and support them, helping them to make better progress.

If we don't circulate, we risk missing out on important and useful information such as this.

There we have eleven techniques through which to elicit information. The list is not exhaustive but it should give you a good starting point. Next, we turn to effective feedback.

Effective feedback

There are three ways in which we can use the information we elicit about our students' thinking and learning:

- To adapt and modify our teaching
- To adapt and modify our planning
- To provide effective feedback.

Here we will concentrate on the third of these.

Effective feedback is formative. In that respect it gives students a sense of what they have done well and what they need to do to improve.

It is also personal to the pupil in question. That does not mean we need to write or say something completely different to every student we teach. Plainly this is not the case seeing as how many pupils struggle with the same things or need to make similar improvements.

Assessment in the round

What it does mean is that the feedback is relevant – it connects to what the pupil has done, what they have thought or what they have produced.

Finally, effective feedback is clear and precise. These two points are true of effective communication in general. Without clarity and precision we risk failing to convey that which we wanted to convey. In the context of feedback this is doubly problematic because not only are we expecting students to understand the feedback we give, but we are also expecting them to use the feedback to do things.

To put it another way, we are giving them advice to follow and targets to strive for.

We can break down effective feedback into three categories: verbal, written and non-verbal.

Starting with non-verbal, this invariably involves body language and is often about modifying what students are doing in the moment. So, for example, we might raise an eyebrow to indicate displeasure or we might make a hand gesture to signal that a pupil should carry on explaining.

Non-verbal feedback is important in the classroom but it does not generally play much of a role in facilitating learning.

Verbal and written feedback do, however.

Verbal feedback takes place regularly during lessons. Here are five simple ways to make sure it is based on information you elicit and that it is as effective as possible:

1. Ask questions to individual students in order to gauge their understanding of what you are studying or what it is you have asked them to do. Having done this, provide verbal feedback explicitly tied to what they have said.

2. During a lesson, circulate through the room. Stop and read the work of pupils who you think would benefit from some support at this point. Having read their work, provide brief, specific advice, accompanied by an example, which shows them what they need to do to improve.

3. When students are working on an activity – either individually or in groups – call certain pupils up to the front of the room. Talk to them about the work and the learning. Then, provide feedback based on what they have said. This feedback could focus on the task in hand or it could be about the learning more generally.

4. At the end of a lesson, ask a student or a couple of students to stay behind. Give them some feedback about how they could improve next time based on the information you have elicited concerning their learning during the course of the lesson.

5. During a discussion activity, join a pair or group who are discussing. Take part in their conversation and use the opportunity to provide feedback which is relevant to what they are talking about and the knowledge and understanding which underpins this.

Written feedback tends not to take place during lessons. Instead, it tends to be created by the teacher outside of lessons. Students then read it and act on it when they are in the classroom. Here are five methods you can use to ensure written feedback is effective:

1. Place a target tracker sheet in the front of pupils' books. This is a sheet of A4 paper on which there are boxes where you can write the targets you set for your students. The great advantage of this approach is that you and your pupils can keep track of targets over time. In particular, this allows you to identify whether the information you are eliciting is the same or different over weeks, months or terms.

2. Provide students with two or three strengths and one target. The strengths will help them to understand what they have done well and will also make it easier to take on board constructive criticism.

3. Always stick to one target. I repeat this here because it is vital to facilitating success. Multiple targets pull us in different directions. This diminishes the power of the mind because our

attention is not focused on one single thing. The result is that students will struggle to achieve any of the targets and will feel uncertain as to what exactly they should be aiming towards.

4. Give written feedback at particular points in the term. You can then spend the weeks leading up to this eliciting the relevant information. This way, your written feedback is based on what happens during lessons as well as what students produce in any formal assessment.

5. In the lesson when pupils get their written feedback, set aside time in which they can reflect on this and make their first attempts at putting it into practice. This way, you ensure that the feedback has an immediate effect and that you are on hand to offer advice and guidance to any students who are not sure what their feedback means.

In all the methods outlined above, for both written and verbal feedback, two key points can be seen.

First, effective feedback is closely tied to the eliciting of relevant information – that is, information which tells us about students' learning and thinking.

Second, effective feedback is focused, specific and tied to the pupil in question. It is self-evident why this type of feedback will lead to the most significant learning gains.

Opening up success criteria

The final element of assessment we need to think about is that of opening up success criteria.

Success criteria are those things against which students' work is judged. They include mark-schemes, levelling information and the general criteria we as teachers possess about what constitutes good work – both in general and in relation to specific subjects and topics.

By opening up success criteria we allow pupils to better understand what it is their work is being judged against. This, in turn, means that students have a better idea of what they need to do in order to be successful.

In one sense then, here we are turning the elicitation of information on its head. Instead of continuing to focus on how we can elicit and use information, we are thinking about how to provide pupils with the information they need to use if they are to have the best chance of being successful.

As such, there is a nice symmetry with what we have previously said.

However, there is also a sense in which opening up success criteria aids our overarching goal of seeking to elicit and use information about students' thinking and learning.

If we open up success criteria, then we place pupils in a stronger position. They no longer have to guess or assume what they need to do to be successful. As a result, they are likely to produce work which more closely matches the demands of the particular task on which they are working.

The consequence of this fact is that when we come to assess the work that pupils produce, we will be able to give them feedback which helps them to better meet the success criteria or, even, move beyond them.

In short, we are speeding up the process of progression. By providing the success criteria, we are actually giving students a piece of general feedback from the word 'go'. That is: here are the things you need to do to be successful. Now you can work towards them in order to do well.

This places us in an enviable position. We are able to elicit information concerning our students' thinking and learning which is closely tied to the success criteria their work is judged against. Doing this continually makes for a highly effective feedback–progress loop.

Here are five simple ways through which you can share success criteria with students:

1. When you set a task or activity, display a collection of success criteria on the board. Three or five is usually the right amount.

These criteria should be short, specific and easy for pupils to follow. You might like to spend a couple of minutes explaining them before the task begins.

2.   Hand out slips of paper containing the success criteria for the current task. There are two advantages to this. First, students can keep them close while they are working. This makes it easier for them to refer to these during the task. Second, you can personalise the success criteria if you wish, giving more challenging ones to pupils who are more able.

3.   If you are teaching an exam class, provide students with copies of the mark-scheme examiners use. They can then use this while they plan and produce their work.

4.   If your pupils are already familiar with success criteria, you can begin a task by having a discussion with them during which you as a class come up with your own success criteria. The benefit here is that students are encouraged to think actively about the nature of success in relation to the lesson. They will also have to justify and defend any ideas they put forward.

5.   Provide pupils with copies of exemplar work in which it is clearly exemplified how one goes about meeting the success criteria. Students can then use these as models – starting off points – from which to begin their own work and their own search for success.

Another means through which to open up success criteria – one we mentioned briefly earlier on – is through the use of self- and peer-assessment activities.

Self-assessment involves students assessing their own work in the light of some set of criteria. Peer-assessment involves pupils doing the same thing for the work of one of their peers.

In both cases, the success criteria are opened up and made explicit. This is because pupils have to use them and think about them in order to successfully apply them. If you use one or both of the approaches routinely, students will come to internalise both the processes and the criteria which animate them.

Here are three quick self-assessment techniques:

- Students complete a piece of work and then assess it using the success criteria before handing it in.

- As above except, this time, pupils assess their work in light of their most recent target. The purpose here is to ascertain whether or not sufficient progress is being made.

- The teacher asks students to read through their work and then to identify two stars and a wish. The stars are things the pupil has done well. The wish is something they wish they could do better next time.

And here are three quick peer-assessment techniques:

- Students swap their work with a partner. They then mark the work using the success criteria before returning it and discussing their judgement with their partner.

- The teacher collects the class's work in, shuffles this and then redistributes it at random. Pupils peer-assess whatever work they receive, using the success criteria. They then find the author and talk them through the judgements they have made.

- Students leave their work open on their desks. Two-thirds of the class are strength-spotters and one-third are target-givers. Pupils walk around the room giving out strengths and targets. The teacher indicates that, by the end of the activity, every book should have two strengths and one target written in it.

With that we conclude our journey through assessment. The emphasis has been on seeing assessment in the round: as a continuous process centred on learning. This has helped us to understand what Habit One: Eliciting and Using Information looks like in practice. Now we move on to habit two!

5 Planning for progress

Habit Two: Facilitating Progress

Progress is the aim of all teaching. By progress, we mean learning. By learning we mean being able to do more and knowing more than was previously the case.

Outstanding teaching sees students making excellent progress. This means they learn a lot, in terms of skills and content, lesson after lesson. For this reason, pupils who experience outstanding teaching tend to achieve more highly. This is a result of the accumulated learning gains they make over the course of their school life.

In terms of our habits, this chapter connects to Habit Two: Facilitating Progress.

Facilitating progress means doing everything possible to ensure learning happens. It also means seeking to maximise the amount of learning that happens. In this way, lessons are not just good but outstanding.

Before we go on to look at the specific things on which we can focus to facilitate great progress, let us attend to the term itself in a little more detail.

To progress means to get better, to advance and to develop. In the context of the classroom we are frequently exhorted to 'show progress' or to ensure that progress is happening across the board.

It is fair to say that, to some extent, use and misuse of the word 'progress' has resulted in a degree of uncertainty arising in teachers' minds. Many have questioned precisely what it means and, in so doing, have made plain a worry that they have about how the term actually connects to what goes on in the classroom.

That worry is understandable. It stems from a lack of clarity regarding what the word means when used in the context of observations and so forth. Here we can dispel this concern, providing ourselves with a firm base from which to move forwards.

Progress means that students have learned. This learning could be in the form of increased knowledge, better understanding or greater proficiency in the use of skills. Generally, progress will encompass two or three of these things at the same time.

And that is it. No secret. No huge explanation. Progress means learning. Maximising progress means maximising learning. The best way in which to ensure this happens is to plan effectively. That is, to plan with progress in mind.

So doing will help you to ensure that every aspect of your teaching is set up to facilitate the progress of your students.

How do we plan for progress?

Lesson planning is one of the teacher's core tasks, along with teaching lessons and marking. It is through our planning that we create the situations in which learning can happen. Planning leads to progress. Without it, we have a much lower chance of successfully facilitating the growth and development of our students.

Later on in this chapter we will look at the special role of Bloom's Taxonomy in planning for progress. We will also consider how the points raised in the previous chapter, about assessment, can be harnessed in order to help us to plan for progress.

First, we will look at five other aspects of lesson planning which can help us achieve this end.

1 Lesson structure

The lesson structure is the overarching framework into which your lesson fits. In the United Kingdom, the most common structure is the three-part lesson. This involves a starter activity, one or more main activities and a plenary.

The popularity of this method can be traced back to changes in the government's approach to teaching and learning in the late 1990s and early 2000s. During this time, the inspection framework for schools became more prescriptive; included in this was a focus on the three-part lesson.

Regardless of its origins, the three-part lesson is here to stay.

This is no bad thing seeing as how the structure is designed to promote and secure progress.

Starter activities are intended to grab and engage students, giving them an opportunity to experience success early in the lesson.

Main activities involve pupils manipulating and engaging with the content which forms the basis of the learning.

Plenary activities offer a chance to review, revisit and reinforce the learning which has taken place.

While other lesson structures are available – many of which are also conducive to the securing of great progress – there is no doubt that the popularity of the three-part lesson stems in no small part from the way in which it simplifies the planning process while, at the same time, keeping the lesson's entire focus on the facilitation of progress.

We will now consider each aspect of the three-part lesson in turn.

2 Starter activities

These come at the beginning of lessons. In terms of progress, they serve a number of ends.

First, they offer a means through which to quickly bind students into the lesson. Second, they present pupils with an opportunity to experience success right away. This creates positive connotations and a sense of confidence that the learning can be accessed. Third, they give the teacher an opportunity to assess what is already known (and this information can then be used to adapt and develop the rest of the lesson).

(For a wide variety of starter activities based on these principles, see my free resource The Starter Generator at www.mikegershon. com.)

3 Main activities

The main activities are where most of the learning happens. Therefore, they provide the key opportunity for progress to take place. It is here that students come into contact with new ideas and information, practise skills and create products which reflect what they know and what they can do.

How many activities you use is up to you. Rather than being guided by a specific number or a certain style of activity (lengthy or episodic) it is better to select your activities based on the facilitation of progress.

So, for example, while planning your lesson you should consider:

1. How your different activities fit together.

2. How your first activity leads into the second, the second into the third and so on.

3. How your activities present an increasing degree of challenge (for more on which, see below).

These three points are important because we need to create a main activity section which has coherence (1), which has a logical flow (2) and which presents our students with a steadily increasing degree of challenge (3).

This last point is particularly important. If we are to sustain progress through a lesson – and therefore maximise the amount of learning which takes place – we need to ensure that at every point students are having their thinking pushed. If this is not the case, it is likely that progress will be uneven across the lesson and, therefore, that we will miss out on the potential learning gains we could have achieved with a more coherent and gradually challenging set of activities.

(For a wide range of activities suitable for use in any lesson, take a look at my free resources, The Ultimate Lesson Activity Generator and The Discussion Toolkit, available at the above website.)

4 Plenaries

Plenaries come at the end of lessons. They involve the manipulation of prior learning. This is done with the intention that students reflect on their learning – revisiting it and reinforcing it in the process.

The purpose behind plenaries is to go over that which has been learned, thus increasing pupils' familiarity with it and promoting the development of metacognition (thinking about thinking).

You can also use plenaries during lessons as review opportunities. Including these means giving yourself a chance to quickly elicit information about where your class are at in terms of their learning; you can then use this information to adapt your teaching.

The structure of plenaries is simple: students are asked to manipulate their prior learning through some task or cognitive process. For example: identify (process) three things you have learned this lesson (prior learning).

(For a wealth of ready-to-use plenaries, see my free resources The Plenary Producer and Plenaries on a Plate.)

5 Post-lesson reflection

Each of the elements outlined above are integral to the maximisation of progress in a lesson. A good starter, designed to get students thinking and experiencing success, followed by a selection of increasingly challenging main activities, topped off by a reflective and engaging plenary will see pupils learning continuously throughout the lesson.

What is more, this learning will be at a high level, based as it is on well-chosen, relevant and stimulating lesson elements.

This whole process is planning in a nutshell. But what comes after is equally as important.

Having taught a lesson, we should spend time reflecting on how it went – what happened and whether things turned out as we expected or not.

This period of critical evaluation can be anything from a few minutes to half an hour, depending on the lesson itself. Usually it will be closer to the former.

The process of reflection sees the teacher analysing and assessing the results of their planning so that they might improve matters in the future. This improvement could be in relation to the specific lesson, to the class or to the lesson planning in general.

Whatever impact it has, the point is the same. Post-lesson reflections allow for continuous improvement which, in turn, serves to further maximise student progress over time.

Progress and assessment

We looked at assessment in detail in the last chapter. Here we can consider it more explicitly in terms of planning and, specifically, planning for progress.

As we noted, eliciting and using information is central to outstanding teaching.

We also commented that it is important to consider while planning how we might best elicit information during the course of our lessons and as regards formal assessments.

Here we will look at some practical activities you can include as part of your planning, in order to secure maximum progress across the board.

Implementing targets: three simple methods

When we give students formative feedback we provide them with targets. These targets indicate what pupils need to do to improve. Targets only have their desired effect if we give students the opportunity to put them into practice. The best way to do this is to plan for it. That way, we can be certain that we are including the necessary activities in our lessons.

Here are three methods you can use.

Method one: write; do; reflect

Students write their target out at the beginning of a piece of work. They then attempt to put that target into practice through the course of their work. Finally, they write a paragraph reflecting on the extent to which they have been successful.

You can plan this method into your lessons quite easily. It is best used reasonably soon after you have provided pupils with a new target. It is a method you can use again and again, encouraging students to continue putting their targets into practice over a series of lessons.

As you will note, the approach sees students thinking actively about their targets on three different levels. First, they must attend to them when writing them out. Second, they must think about them while producing their work. Third, they must reflect on them in light of what they have done.

Method two: feedback directly prior to a formal assessment

This method again requires you to think about assessment in the context of your planning.

Decide when you are going to give students a formal assessment to complete. Then, plan to assess the work they have been producing in lessons a week or two before this. As part of this assessment you can provide them with a target they need to work on in the formal assessment.

The purpose here is to incorporate the quest for progress and development into any formal assessments we use. This way, those assessments become a formative as well as a summative experience. Not only can we gain a summary of what students know, understand and have learned, but so too can students use the opportunity to continue improving and developing.

This sees us making a subtle change to the traditional nature of formal assessments. We are turning them into an opportunity for making progress as well as a chance to check and assess what students know and have learned.

Method three: schedule formative marking

Formative marking provides pupils with guidance on their learning – where they are at and where they need to go.

For this reason, it takes longer to do than summative marking. Writing a letter or number on twenty-five pieces of work is much quicker than writing a couple of detailed sentences.

The risk is that the extra demands made on our time by formative marking may cause us to eschew it on occasion, or to feel overwhelmed.

You can avoid both of these issues by planning in advance when you will do your formative marking.

This way, you avoid having to do a lot of marking at the same time. In addition, you can look to fit your marking into periods during the term when you have more free time or fewer urgent issues with which to deal. For example, if you are involved in the Christmas show, it would be a good idea not to plan any formative marking for the week of the performance.

This method is thus about managing your own time effectively so as to ensure you can regularly give high-quality formative feedback to all the students you teach, throughout the year.

The final point we will make here regarding progress and assessment is that it is always a good idea to plan a series of assessments over the course of the year through which you can gain a regular summative overview of where your students are at.

The purpose here is twofold.

First, by planning assessments across an entire year, you provide a sense of structure to your teaching. This is because you will be teaching and planning lessons with the assessments in mind. While I am not advocating focusing all your teaching on the assessments, it would be churlish to suggest that we should do anything other than pay special attention to the means through which we will judge where pupils are at.

Furthermore, it is through regular summative assessment that we can track the progress pupils are making in an administrative sense. We do not need to share this data with pupils other than at pre-defined points in the year, because they will be focusing on their formative feedback instead.

However, the summative grades you collect will act as a powerful form of information you can use to ascertain how your students are doing compared to your expectations, who might need more help and support, and what kind of impact your teaching is having across an extended period. All these things are much harder to judge without having the information provided by a series of pre-planned formal assessments.

Second, planning your assessments in advance allows you to get a clear sense in your own mind of the path you are expecting progress to take, for your students, over the course of the year.

This simple technique means you will always have a wider structure to which you can refer; and this will help to guide you in the more specific things you do both in terms of individual lesson planning and the teaching you deliver.

Progress and lesson planning

We turn now from the general to the specific, such that we might focus on the things you can do to secure progress when planning lessons.

Our first approach involves the use of Bloom's Taxonomy of Educational Objectives. The taxonomy was put together in the

1960s by a group of American educators and academics. Its purpose was to delineate the separate skills or processes which form a part of teaching and then to rank these in a hierarchy.

This led to a conception of mastery learning. By progressing up the hierarchy in relation to some particular content, a student gradually comes to master that content.

For our purposes, we are concerned with the first part of the taxonomy: that dealing with the cognitive domain.

The levels are as follows:

- Level 1 – Knowledge
- Level 2 – Comprehension
- Level 3 – Application
- Level 4 – Analysis
- Level 5 – Synthesis
- Level 6 – Evaluation

The levels get progressively more challenging. Clearly it is easier to recall the meaning (level 1 – knowledge) of nuclear fusion than assess the strengths and weaknesses of the method (level 6 – evaluation) as a means through which to generate energy.

Similarly, it is harder to plan your own system of legislative government (level 5 – synthesis) than it is to read a summary of the one which presently exists in the United Kingdom (level 2 – comprehension).

This illustrates the fact that the taxonomy is inherently progressive. Travelling up through the levels leads to growth and development. This process can be conceived of as the development of mastery. That mastery being over some specific content or skill.

To reinforce the point, note how we need to be able to fulfil the lower levels of the taxonomy before we can engage with the higher ones.

We simply cannot analyse or evaluate something we do not first know and, at least to some degree, understand.

Planning for progress

Bloom's Taxonomy is thus a brilliant tool on which we can call when planning lessons and when planning individual segments of lessons. We can apply the structure of the taxonomy so as to ensure our lessons remain consistently challenging, continuously pushing students' thinking in pursuit of mastery.

In a moment, we will outline a range of ways in which you might do this. Before we do, Figure 5.1 gives a visualisation of the taxonomy along with a set of keywords connecting to each level.

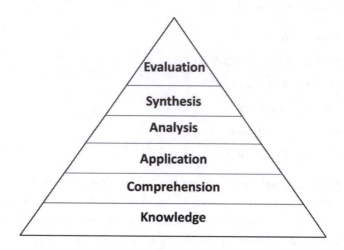

Figure 5.1 Bloom's Taxonomy of Educational Objectives

Bloom's keywords:

Knowledge: Arrange, Define, Describe, List, Match, Memorise, Name, Order, Quote, Recall, Recognise, Repeat, Reproduce, Restate, Retain.

Comprehension: Characterise, Classify, Complete, Describe, Discuss, Establish, Explain, Express, Identify, Illustrate, Recognise, Relate, Report, Sort, Translate.

Application: Apply, Calculate, Choose, Demonstrate, Dramatise, Employ, Implement, Interpret,

	Operate, Perform, Practise, Role Play, Sketch, Solve, Suggest.
Analysis:	Analyse, Appraise, Categorise, Compare, Contrast, Differentiate, Discriminate, Distinguish, Examine, Experiment, Explore, Investigate, Question, Research, Test.
Synthesis:	Combine, Compose, Construct, Create, Design, Devise, Formulate, Hypothesise, Integrate, Merge, Organise, Plan, Propose, Synthesise, Unite.
Evaluation:	Appraise, Argue, Assess, Critique, Defend, Evaluate, Examine, Grade, Inspect, Judge, Justify, Rank, Rate, Review, Value.

Bloom's Taxonomy planning techniques

1 Lesson objectives

You can use Bloom's Taxonomy to establish your lesson objectives. To secure great progress, we should always aim to choose keywords from higher up the taxonomy around which to base our objectives. This will ensure that our lessons drive towards a high degree of mastery.

So, for example, you might select an objective such as: to be able to *assess* the costs and benefits of increased tourism. Using the higher levels of the taxonomy to underpin your objectives means you will be able to frame your entire lesson so that it aims for significant progress.

2 Lesson outcomes

Similarly, we can use the taxonomy to define our outcomes. These are the specific things we want students to be able to do. If they can do these, then they will have achieved the objective. Outcomes are essentially the delineation of the objective in practical terms.

Planning for progress

If you opt for the all/most/some approach (all students will be able to . . . ; most students will be able to . . . ; some students will be able to . . .), then you can use different levels of the taxonomy for each of these outcomes. That way, you can ensure that the outcomes are progressively challenging. This, again, helps to embed a focus on continuous progress in your lesson planning.

3 Individual activities

We can call on the levels of the taxonomy when designing and selecting the activities we use in lessons.

As we noted earlier, good starter activities allow students to experience success, thus helping to motivate and engage them. It makes sense to centre starter activities on the first two levels of the taxonomy – knowledge and comprehension – as these are the simplest cognitive processes. Therefore, they are the ones which students will find easiest to access.

Progressing through the lesson, you can seek to base your activities around increasingly higher levels of the taxonomy. So, for example, you might move from an application activity to an analysis activity and then, finally, to an evaluation activity.

Planning activities in this way means using the taxonomy as a tool through which to structure the learning which happens in your lessons. This helps to ensure that the emphasis is always on progress and development – never will there be a possibility that the learning is losing pace or challenge, because moving up the levels of the taxonomy means this cannot happen.

4 Sections of individual activities

It is even possible to link together different levels of Bloom's Taxonomy within an individual activity. This allows us to maximise progress on an activity-by-activity basis, as well as through the lesson as a whole.

Here is an example:

Subject: English

Task: First read through the poem and talk to your partner about what you think it might mean. When you have done this, see if you can identify 3 examples of strong imagery, onomatopoeia or metaphor. Then, discuss these examples with your partner and decide to what extent they add to the meaning the poem is trying to convey, or whether they actually take away from its purpose.

Here we have combined knowledge and comprehension in the first part of the task, followed by application in the second and then evaluation in the third. As a result, we have built progress into an individual activity.

Doing this throughout a lesson and tying it into a wider movement through the taxonomy means you will be setting your students up to make sustained and consistent progress.

5 Questions

The keywords outlined above are a perfect tool for use in the creation of questions. Simply take words from the levels in which you are interested and use these to form your questions. These could be verbal questions or they could be written ones.

In the former case, you can use different levels of the taxonomy to create questions tailored to the student with whom you are talking. In the latter case, you can create a series of questions connected to a task which get progressively more challenging.

Equally, you can use the higher levels of the taxonomy to develop overarching questions and enquiry questions which will direct the learning which goes on in your lessons. Again, this will help to embed challenge and a clear sense of progression.

6 Extension tasks

We will look at personalising learning in greater detail in the next chapter. However, while on the topic of Bloom's Taxonomy, we can note that it provides a great tool for use in the creation of extension questions and tasks.

These are the questions and tasks you use to push students' thinking after they have finished the main body of work. These might be aimed at the most-able students in your class, or they might be designed to be challenging and yet accessible to everybody.

Either way, the keywords associated with synthesis and evaluation will provide you with fertile ground from which to develop suitably engaging tasks and questions.

7 Formal assessments

Analysis of most GCSE and A Level mark-schemes will show the footprint of Bloom's Taxonomy. This manifests itself in the sense that the higher marks are received for evidence of the processes which are at the top of the taxonomy, whereas the lower marks are awarded for those closer to the bottom.

You can use Bloom's Taxonomy to structure any formal assessment you create for the students you teach. This way, you can be sure that the assessments get progressively more challenging, that they push the thinking of your pupils and, most importantly, that that which you are working towards represents a goal which is stimulating and predicated on pupils making excellent progress (after all, if they don't make excellent progress, how will they be able to successfully complete the higher aspects of the assessment?).

8 Effective formative feedback

When planning and writing your formative feedback, you can call on the taxonomy to help you ensure that it maximises progress. For example, if a pupil is struggling to come to terms with an idea, you can offer them a target based on the level of analysis, knowing full well that subsequent to this you will push them to develop their skills of synthesis and then evaluation.

In this way, the taxonomy can be used to underpin and, to some extent, help you to plan the feedback you give to pupils.

9 Success criteria

In the last chapter we noted the importance of success criteria. They help pupils to understand what they need to do in order to be successful – as well as what it is their work will be judged against.

You can use Bloom's Taxonomy to underpin the success criteria you share with students. If your success criteria progress up the taxonomy, then they will be inherently progressive, meaning your pupils will make more and more progress simply by meeting each one in turn.

In each of the nine practical applications of Bloom's Taxonomy we have explained, one point remains true: we take the taxonomy and use it to structure something we do as part of our planning, our assessment or our teaching.

Responding within lessons

At first glance it might seem odd that I have included this section within the chapter on planning. Allow me to explain.

In any lesson, things will happen which will cause us to change that which we planned. This is to be expected and is an integral feature of outstanding teaching. As we noted in the previous chapter, the point of eliciting information is to then be in a position to use that information for the benefit of our students.

So, we can say without question that, invariably, we will need to adapt and change what we do while we are teaching.

In terms of planning for progress, two points suggest themselves.

First, we should make sure that we are ready for the possibility that we will need to change and adapt. If we do not set ourselves up with this expectation, then there is a strong likelihood we will fail to take advantage of situations as and when they arise. This will be to our detriment and to the detriment of our students as well.

Second, if we are prepared for the possibility that we will need to change and adapt, we can then plan in such a way as to give ourselves the space and slack we need to make the necessary changes with ease. What is more, we will be able to anticipate some of these changes in advance (for example, simplifying tasks, providing further extension work and so forth).

The point here is that when we are planning for progress, we need to attend to our own mental states as well as the actual lessons we prepare.

Being wedded to a detailed, exceptionally well-planned lesson will cause you to miss opportunities through which to facilitate progress; your concentration will be on your attempt to make that which you planned a reality. In fact, it should be on what is happening in front of you – the actual learning in which students are engaging.

Here is an example to illustrate the point.

Imagine we plan a lesson for a Year Seven class on rights and responsibilities. We produce a detailed lesson plan, create an amazing PowerPoint and build some fantastic resources, with all of this being underpinned by Bloom's Taxonomy.

Upon delivering the lesson we quickly realise that we have overestimated the prior knowledge of our students.

Now, if we remain wedded to the plan, we will end up teaching a lesson in which we are continually struggling to get students to access work that is, at this point, just that bit beyond them. As a result, the progress pupils make will be far less than it could have been.

If we approach the lesson with an expectation that things like this might occur, a different situation will play out. Here, we will adapt the lesson as soon as we realise we have overestimated the pupils' prior knowledge. We will take a step back, work to bridge the knowledge gap and only then return to the activities and materials we had previously planned.

In this second example we can see that students would make far more progress. This would be a direct result of the teacher's flexibility and their decision to enter the classroom with an open mind, with the expectation that they might have to adapt and alter their plans in light of the information they elicit from their students.

We can see the temptation is to always assume that by planning high-quality lessons designed to facilitate great progress we have done our job; and that that is the end of it. The reality is different. Outstanding planning includes preparing for change, both in terms of adjusting our mindsets and expectations and in terms of thinking in advance of some of the ways in which we might best respond to changes which present themselves.

On occasions, it can even prove necessary to throw everything we have planned out of the window. The need for such extreme behaviour is rare, but it does happen. And when it does, it is clear to see that trying to plough on out of sheer bloody-mindedness with the lesson we have planned is of no help to anybody.

Progress takes care of itself

We bring this chapter to a close by turning to the influential and inspiring thoughts of Bill Walsh, set down for all to read in his book *The Score Takes Care of Itself* (2010), written with Steve Jamison and Craig Walsh.

Bill Walsh was head coach of the American football team the San Francisco 49ers. He took the team from the very bottom of the pile to the very top in only a few years and then kept them there. The 49ers remained near the top of the game in the years after he left the organisation as well.

In *The Score Takes Care of Itself*, Walsh outlines the lessons he has learned about leadership. These relate closely to what he did during his time in San Francisco.

Central to Walsh's message is the idea that if you keep your focus on getting every aspect of your work and your organisation right, if you ensure all the people you work with know exactly what they need to do and how they can do it to the highest standards possible, then the score (in his case, the football score) will take care of itself.

The argument is about putting the end goal to one side and focusing instead on every element which might contribute to that goal.

Planning for progress

The logic is clear. The goal is in fact a result of the things which came before. We are unlikely to achieve the goal if we constantly obsess over it. What we need to do is devote our attention to the things which lead towards the goal. By focusing on these we are taking practical steps towards what we want to achieve.

By trying to make every single part of what we do outstanding, we can be fairly confident that the score will look after itself. It must do; this is a logical deduction.

If the score is a function of all the things we do to get towards it, then doing those things superbly and paying close attention to them at all times will result in the score (or the goal) being achieved.

If we translate this to a classroom context we can see that a relentless focus on progress will not be particularly helpful. In fact, it may even be counter-productive.

Progress is the end towards which we are working but it is not the means through which we get there. Everything we have mentioned in this chapter – and that which can be found elsewhere in this book – is the means. By focusing on getting these things right, the progress students make will take care of itself.

Remembering this while you are planning, teaching and marking will do two things.

First, it will help to reassure you that you are indeed expending your energy in the direction of the end you desire.

Second, it will help you to recall how important it is to make each habit of outstanding teaching a part of your daily practice – because by doing this, and by doing it consistently, you can rest assured that the progress will take care of itself.

6 Personalising the journey

Habit Three: Personalising Learning

Personalising the journey is all about differentiation. It's about finding the things you can do to help all pupils access the learning and to ensure all pupils have their thinking stretched and challenged.

Linking back to the last chapter, it's about finding ways to make sure all students make the most progress possible.

As we noted in Chapter 2, differentiation can be broken down into five categories:

- Activities
- Questioning
- Words and writing
- Things the teacher can do or use
- Things you can ask students to do or use.

In this chapter we will look at how you can embed the habit of personalising learning in your teaching. In so doing, we will draw examples from each of these categories, making clear some of the practical strategies, activities and techniques you can put to use in your lessons.

How do we personalise the journey?

It is not possible to personalise every single thing we do in the classroom. Nor is it feasible to create a collection of different lessons or resources aimed at the same group of students but pitched at different levels so as to match their current knowledge and understanding.

These things are neither possible nor feasible for the simple fact that they are not practical.

In teaching, as in life, our time is limited. Therefore, we need to find ways in which to achieve our objectives which are both realistic and attainable.

Looking at the issue from another angle, we should also note that it is not desirable to personalise every single thing for every student, or to create myriad different lessons and resources. If we did do this, we would be sending a message to our pupils that went something like this: 'Everything will be tailored to your exact needs and requirements, so expect it to be like this, now and in the future.'

Such a message would not stimulate the habits of outstanding learning we outlined in Chapter 3. In fact, it would actively militate against them.

Personalising learning is thus about finding effective and efficient ways through which we can ensure access and through which we can stretch and challenge the thinking of all pupils.

By first accepting the limits of what is possible we can then start to develop and employ strategies which work.

Here we will explain a range of these, based on the five categories noted above.

Activities

Differentiated activities are those which all students can access and which push the thinking of all pupils. By designing such activities you can ensure that differentiation is built into your planning.

What is more, you will only need to develop one set of activities per lesson – as opposed to a variety, each targeted at different groups of students.

Further benefits accrue over time. Having designed some high-quality differentiated activities, you can then use these again in future lessons. Remember, activities are vessels into which different content can be placed. As such, they can be transposed from lesson to lesson.

Here are three examples of differentiated activities which also illustrate this point about vessels for content.

Activity: Options

In this activity, we present the class with a selection of options through which to engage with the content. These options are of varying degrees of difficulty. Students self-select, with the teacher circulating through the room so as to ensure no one has chosen an option which is clearly too easy for them. Here is an example of the activity:

Stimulus: 'History should see Henry VIII as a bad king'

Task: Choose one of the following options through which to respond to the statement:

   i.   Write an essay outlining the arguments for and against.

   ii. Create a storyboard showing a TV documentary examining the statement.

   iii. Produce an imaginary interview between you and Henry VIII in which you put this statement to him.

   iv. Work with a partner to design a poster advertising and explaining your views on the statement.

   v.   Evaluate the arguments for and against the statement and then use this information to produce your own interpretation of Henry's reign.

97

Personalising the journey

As you can see, all the options encourage students to engage with the content in challenging ways. However, some of the options are more difficult than others. Presenting an activity such as this means giving pupils choice over how they think about and interact with the material. This means we have an activity which is automatically differentiated.

While I have used a History example here, the same model can be applied to any subject. The purpose is simply to provide students with a range of options from which they can select how they will engage with the task.

Activity: Design Brief

This activity sees you providing students with a task they have to complete alongside a set of instructions for the completion of that task. These instructions are general rather than specific. In essence they are success criteria (see Chapter 4) which pupils need to fulfil in order to produce excellent work. Here is an example:

Task: Create a solution to the problem of climate change.

Instructions:
- Your solution should include information about a minimum of two renewable energy sources.
- You should provide an explanation of the threats climate change poses.
- You should suggest at least two ways, one large scale and one small scale, through which we could decrease the amount of energy our society uses.

The activity provides pupils with a structure and then invites them to respond to this structure to the best of their abilities. It takes students a certain distance and then asks them to complete the rest of the work themselves.

Here, effective personalisation is again secured by providing pupils with a framework and then inviting them to make choices and decisions within that framework. In so doing, they deal with the task in a way which is personal to them and which reflects their current knowledge and understanding.

As with 'options', the design brief model can be adapted to fit any lesson or any topic. It is simply a case of swapping the task and the instructions to suit your particular aim.

Activity: Stepped Activities

These are activities which contain a series of steps. The steps are progressively more challenging. All the steps are open to all pupils. However, it may be the case that only certain students will complete all the steps; others will get so far along and then find the work sufficiently challenging to warrant stopping there. Here is an example:

Topic: The Digestive System

Steps:

i.   Create a diagram showing the main features of the human digestive system.

ii. Annotate your diagram with explanations of how the different parts work.

iii. Identify a problem which may develop within the digestive system. Explain how this might happen and what effects it might have.

iv. Compare the human digestive system to the digestive system of another animal. How is it similar and different? What might be the reasons for this?

v.   What are the strengths and weaknesses of the digestive system?

In this example, each step is more challenging than the last. They roughly mirror the levels of Bloom's Taxonomy (See Chapter 5). Some pupils will be able to complete all five steps. Some students may get to step three and then no further. Through this, we see differentiation happening.

Personalising the journey

Similar to the two previous examples, here the activity is designed so students have choice, are challenged throughout and, as a result, progress is maximised across the class as a whole.

Again, this model can be adapted to fit almost any topic.

Summary points regarding activities

Before we move on to our next section, let me draw your attention to the underlying points these examples illustrate regarding differentiated activities:

1. The activities demonstrate how giving pupils the opportunity to make choices within a given structure facilitates differentiation.

2. They show how paying attention to the nature of your activities allows you to differentiate through your planning.

3. They make clear the fact that differentiation can be achieved through a single activity rather than a range of different ones aimed at different groups of students.

4. They show how activities are frequently vessels for content; they present us with models we can apply in different contexts and with different content.

5. They illustrate how it is possible to use a single activity to continually stretch and challenge the thinking of all students in a class.

You can use these three activities in your own planning. You can also use them, along with the points noted above, as a basis through which to develop your own differentiated activities.

Questioning

We move now to look at questioning and how we can use this important aspect of teaching in order to personalise learning.

The first point to note is that questioning can take one of three forms. First, it can be written, as in the questions we include in tasks and which we use as the basis for lessons. Second, it can be verbal and directed at a number of pupils. For example, when we pose a question to the whole class and then ask students to discuss it with their partners. Third, it can be verbal and directed to one student.

Let us look at each of these in turn.

When posing questions in a written form there are two key ways in which we can differentiate. The first is to use open, enquiry-based questions. For example:

- What might be the cause of radiation?

- How might we solve this equation?

- Is it ever possible to do the right thing and get punished?

Open, enquiry-based questions present all students with the opportunity to think and explore the matter at issue. They do this through their structure; it is an inherent feature.

The three questions above exemplify this point. In each case, no student is excluded from thinking about or engaging with the question. The emphasis here is on critical exploration, as opposed to the search for a single, definitive right answer.

Of course, it is expected that open, enquiry-based questions will eventually lead pupils and the class as a whole to good answers. And in some cases these may be single and definitive. But, consider the different message we are sending to the class if we ask the following questions instead of the ones above:

- Who can tell me what causes radiation?

- What is the answer to this equation?

- Can the right thing lead to punishment?

These questions work to close down thought and discussion. They promote the idea that there is an answer 'out there' which the teacher is looking for. This puts a lot of pupils off. They fear getting the answer wrong and so choose not to engage. Such questions may also lead to guessing; underpinned by a sense that only single, definitive answers are acceptable.

Personalising the journey

Another way through which we can differentiate written questions is by posing a series of questions which get progressively more challenging. These can be structured in accordance with Bloom's Taxonomy or through another method (such as from concrete to abstract – see below).

In terms of verbal questioning to the whole class, we can adapt both the methods outlined above, that is, open, enquiry-based questions and a series of questions which get progressively more challenging.

It is when we come to verbal questioning posed to individuals that we find ourselves with much greater opportunity to differentiate.

Here we will outline five ways in which you might do this.

1 Bloom's-based questions

Returning to our theme of using Bloom's Taxonomy to underpin questioning, we can see that it makes sense to use the levels of the taxonomy to shape the questions we ask to individual students.

For example, it may be that one of our pupils is finding it particularly difficult to get to grips with the topic we are teaching. To help them overcome this problem, we can work one-to-one with them, using questions based on the first two or three levels of the taxonomy to help guide them forwards so that they might develop their understanding.

Similarly, we might have a particularly able student who has completed all the work we have set well in advance of their peers. In order to differentiate for this pupil, we could go and discuss the topic with them one-to-one, using questions predicated on the levels of synthesis and evaluation. This would push the thinking of the student, ensuring they continue to be challenged (and, therefore, to make progress).

2 Concrete to abstract

Concrete thinking tends to be easier to access than abstract thinking. Though this is not always the case, it is generally so. The reason is fairly simple. Concrete thought connects to objects and things in the world. Therefore, we have more solid ground on which to find purchase. Abstract thinking tends to concentrate on the nature of things, on ideas and principles. While this relates to the world and to experience, it tends to do so at a distance and is therefore harder to identify with.

Here is an example of a series of questions which run from concrete to abstract:

Concrete

1. How many ducks are in the pond?
2. What colour are the ducks?
3. How are the ducks behaving?
4. What are the relationships between the ducks?
5. What might be influencing the behaviour and relationships of the ducks?
6. Why might the ducks have come to be as they are?
7. Is all human life mirrored in the vagaries of ducks?
8. If ducks could speak, would we understand them?

Abstract

This example neatly illustrates the points we made above. The more concrete questions are tied to the physical world and everyday experience. The more abstract questions undoubtedly connect to this but are also quite far removed.

When questioning pupils one-to-one, you can use the concrete–abstract approach to develop questions most appropriate for the student with whom you are talking. Therefore, you might use more concrete ones with a pupil who is struggling to understand the work and more abstract ones with a pupil who has quickly grasped the main ideas.

As with the use of Bloom's Taxonomy, this is a tool which allows you to shape and adapt questions on the fly, meaning that you can personalise learning during the lesson in direct response to the information you elicit from your pupils.

3 Socratic questioning

Socratic questioning is based on the questioning of Socrates, the Ancient Greek philosopher, which we find in the Dialogues of Plato. Socrates asks four types of questions:

- *Midwife questions.* These help students to give birth to ideas. For example: What do you mean by that? Can you explain that a bit further?

- *Gadfly questions.* These nip away at pupils' thinking. For example: But what exactly does that mean? How would you explain that in another way? Why is that the case?

- *Ignoramus questions.* These see the questioner playing dumb so as to draw out student thinking. For example: I don't understand, can you tell me right from the beginning?

- *Stingray questions.* These pack a jolt, causing pupils to look at things differently. For example: What if everything you just said was untrue? What if you had to completely change your thinking on the issue?

Having these four question types in mind is another way through which you can differentiate.

First, you can use the different question types for different pupils. Second, you can pursue a whole series of questions of this type with more-able students so as to really push their thinking. Third, you can walk around the room and drop in stingray questions so as to stretch and challenge pupils' thinking just when they think they have got to grips with a topic!

4 Work-based questioning

Asking students questions about their work is another good way to personalise learning. Mid-way through an activity, walk around the room and see where pupils are up to. Select a couple of students who you think would benefit from your intervention and question each one in turn.

Focus your questioning on the work the pupils have produced. Ask them questions about why they have done things in this way, what choices and decisions they have made and how they think they could change or develop things as time progresses.

The purpose here is twofold. First, questioning of this type encourages students to think actively and reflect on the work they are doing. This links closely to the habits of outstanding learning we outlined in Chapter 3.

Second, asking questions in this way allows you to personalise learning with relative ease. This is because the questions you ask will be predicated on information you have elicited about the work produced by the student to whom you are talking. Therefore, they cannot but help be personal and specific to that student.

5 Discursive questioning

By discursive questioning we mean questioning which develops a discussion between you and the student. Through this discussion you can explore ideas and information connected to the lesson. This helps the pupil in question to clarify, verbalise and refine their thoughts. It also gives you the opportunity to lead their thinking in certain directions – directions they may not have been able to access themselves.

You can use all the techniques outlined above to facilitate or structure the kind of discussions you have with your students. Or, you can simply ask them what they think about the lesson content and build a discussion organically from there.

This particular technique is often overlooked in the classroom because it can feel rather close to social conversation. However, what we are actually doing with this approach is gently guiding pupils by using the conventions of social discussion to engage them in critical thought and reflection on the topic of study.

Words and writing

We will explore literacy at length in Chapter 9. There, we will look at a wide range of strategies you can use to support and develop the reading, writing, speaking and listening skills of all your pupils.

So as to avoid repetition, we will keep this section fairly brief, focusing on five important ways through which you can personalise learning for all your students in relation to words and writing.

1 Keywords

Keywords are central to all subjects. They form the linguistic basis of disciplines of thought, giving users access to the knowledge associated with those particular areas. For example, in order to think about History, one needs to have some familiarity with the language of the subject. This is even truer in subjects such as Biology and Chemistry where we find ourselves hard pressed to rely on our broader language base.

There are many ways in which you can help your students to access and understand the meaning of keywords. First, you can use antonyms and synonyms to help explain them. This works well if students are already familiar with these. You can use their existing knowledge as a means through which to unlock and situate the meaning of the new keywords.

Second, you can use images to illustrate the meaning of keywords when first introducing them. This helps pupils to access that meaning and also offers a strong visual cue they can use to help remember the meaning.

Third, you can exemplify the use of keywords in context, providing pupils with written or verbal models which they can copy and imitate. After doing this a few times, students will be in a position to use the keywords in their own way.

2 Simple language

A complex idea clearly explained is readily accessible to all.

This should be your mantra when thinking about your own use of language in the classroom. Keeping your language simple – not dumbing down but speaking and writing with precision and clarity of thought – will make it easier for students to understand what it is you mean and to comprehend any ideas or information you are trying to convey.

A good technique involves asking yourself this question whenever you communicate to pupils through speech or writing: can I say this more simply and yet retain the same meaning? If the answer is yes, make the necessary changes. If the answer is no, you have done your job well.

3 Modelling conversation

Discussion is a superb tool for use in the classroom. It helps pupils to verbalise their thoughts and, in so doing, allows them to refine, develop and further articulate these thoughts. As such, discussion, within a clear framework, is always to be welcomed.

One of the problems that can arise with the use of discussion is that students are not certain how to discuss effectively. This can result in them talking or behaving in ways which do not meet your expectations.

A simple remedy sees you modelling the kind of conversation you want to take place. You can model discussion on your own (through role play) or with a student. Either way, you will be providing your class with clear guidance on what they need to do. This will make it easier for all pupils to access the learning and to make the progress you intended them to make.

4 Sentence starters

Examples of sentence starters include:

- In my opinion . . .
- The first thing is . . .
- It was a dark and stormy night . . .

They are a simple way to help pupils begin writing. They overcome the initial reluctance, uncertainty or anxiety students can experience when faced with a blank piece of paper. They nearly always work, helping pupils to engage with the task and, as a result, access the learning.

You can give out sentence starters verbally, you can display them on the board or you can make wall displays containing commonly used ones. Another option involves making a laminated sentence starter hand-out which you give to particular students or make available for the entire class.

5 Writing frames

Writing frames provide pupils with clear, unadulterated guidance regarding how they need to structure a piece of work. For example, if students are writing an essay, we might give them an essay structure as a writing frame. This could work as follows:

- Paragraph one: introduction
- Paragraph two: first argument for
- Paragraph three: second argument for
- Paragraph four: first argument against
- Paragraph five: second argument against
- Paragraph six: conclusion.

A writing frame does some of the work for students. Instead of having to think about what structure they will use and what content they will place into that structure, pupils can focus entirely on the latter.

Splitting up the cognitive work in this way – doing the structural work for students – means pupils can focus all their attention on a single task. This allows them to make maximum use of their minds, resulting in higher-quality writing and, as a consequence, better progress.

Over time it is likely that students will internalise writing frames. This is a further benefit we can gain from their use. The model comes to be understood and remembered, meaning that pupils have learned it and are then in a position to use it again and again, wherever it might be deemed useful.

That concludes our short engagement with words and writing in the context of personalising learning. We will return to the topic in Chapter 9. Before we move on though, we should point out one key feature common to all the strategies outlined above.

In each case, the central point is that the teacher is able to open up access to language – either in terms of meaning or in terms of usage. In so doing, they break down any barriers which might be standing in students' way, preventing them from successfully accessing the learning and making outstanding progress.

Things the teacher can do or use

This category covers those tools which you can use to shape the learning in your classroom, which help you to personalise what takes place and, in so doing, allow you to facilitate progress across the board.

1 Talking

Talking to students is one of the most effective ways through which you can personalise learning. We alluded to this point in the last section when we looked at the use of questioning in a one-to-one context.

When talking to students, we elicit all sorts of information we can use to inform what we do, how we respond and the decisions we take about the lesson more generally. In any case, we will find ourselves in a position to adapt the learning to the needs of the learner.

So, for example, you might spend a couple of minutes talking to a particular student during a group work activity. Doing this will allow you to see where they are at and what they are thinking. You can respond to them in a way which helps them to think better and understand more. You might re-explain an idea, pose a challenging question or ask them to further explain their views.

Personalising the journey

All these options are present any time we talk to pupils. All of them involve personalising learning and making progress happen.

What is more, talking to students gives you a chance to build and sustain rapport. This is good for obvious reasons and good in terms of differentiation. If you develop positive relationships with your students, they will be more likely to respond well to any interventions you make to try to support them.

One option open to you is to try to talk to every student, every lesson, so as to differentiate the learning for them. This may not be practical, however.

An alternative is to aim to talk to every student over a series of lessons. This way, you can be sure that you have given some of your time to each pupil you teach and actively attempted to personalise the learning for all of them through talking.

2 Task mixture

This involves planning a range of tasks over a series of lessons. The purpose here is to provide students with a variety of opportunities through which to access the learning. So, for example, you might use discussion activities in one lesson, group work in another and individual writing in a third.

Or, if it is manageable, you might include a mixture of tasks in every lesson you teach.

Whichever approach you take, the end result will be the same. You will be giving your pupils different routes into the learning, different ways through which they can engage with the lesson content.

This personalises the learning for two reasons.

First, by presenting different routes into the learning you are aiming to play to the strengths of every student in your class. This will help them get to grips with the work and be successful. Second, through using a mixture of tasks you are ensuring that no student is disadvantaged due to the repetition of a task type they particularly dislike – or find particularly difficult to come to terms with.

An added benefit of all this is that variety tends to promote motivation and engagement. We know this to be the case generally and the principle also applies in the classroom.

3 Assessment for learning

We looked into assessment for learning at length in Chapter 4. All we will say here is that eliciting and using information is a sure-fire way through which to personalise learning. This is because the information you elicit tells you about where pupils are at and what they think; and your use of this information sees the learning being adapted to meet students' individual needs.

Many of the strategies and approaches outlined in Chapter 4 can be called on as part of your efforts to embed Habit Three: Personalising Learning in your day-to-day teaching.

4 Narrative

Narrative means storytelling.

Storytelling is at the heart of the human experience. We use stories to make sense of what happens to us and of our lives more generally. When things occur – or when we do things – we use narrative in order to give them meaning.

In one sense, narrative is a tool for ordering and explaining that which happens to us. So, for example, I might describe my day as a story when I am asked how it was. In actual fact, my day was not a story. It was simply a continuous succession of events, with me as the subject who experienced them.

Such a statement is, to some extent, meaningless, because we never think about what happens to us in this way. Instead, we use narrative to explain, convey and understand our experiences.

You can use storytelling as a differentiation device. This sees you explaining complex ideas and information through the use of narrative. Such a process makes it easier for pupils to grasp lesson content. It also makes it easier for them to remember it.

Personalising the journey

These two points are particularly relevant in relation to abstract ideas or information. In these situations, storytelling contextualises that which is abstract, making it more concrete and easier to handle in cognitive terms.

Another way in which you can use narrative to open up and personalise learning is through the use of case studies. These are extended examples in which ideas and information are embedded – the case study is an exemplar story giving students a concrete insight into that which is abstract, complex or difficult to understand.

We will return to the power of narrative in Chapter 10, when we look at explaining in more detail.

5 Thinking time

This is our final example of things the teacher can do or use to personalise learning. However, you can find further strategies, activities and techniques in my free resource The Differentiation Deviser, available at www.mikegershon.com, and in my bestselling book *How to use Differentiation in the Classroom: The Complete Guide* (2013).

Thinking time means asking students a question and then waiting before taking answers. By waiting you give students time to think. Through thinking they will be able to come up with better answers than would otherwise have been the case.

This means they will be able to engage with the learning. It also means you will be able to elicit information which is useful – which you can use to support them, challenge them and through which you can stretch their thinking.

Whenever you ask a question – to individuals, pairs, groups or the whole class – make sure you give pupils time to think about their answers. This will result in far more learning taking place than if you demand a response straight away (which, for whatever reason, tends to be the default position many of us unwittingly fall in to).

Things you can ask students to do or use

We conclude this chapter by turning our attention to pupils. Here we will think about some of the things we can ask them to do or use to help ensure the learning which goes on is personalised.

You will note that some of what we have already looked at overlaps with this category. Not least the activities section.

The great benefit of including this element within your quest for effective differentiation is that it helps you to make pupils pro-active and self-sufficient when it comes to differentiation. To put it another way, these strategies help you to cultivate the habits of outstanding learning.

1 Students teaching

If a student in your class finishes a task in advance of the rest of the group, you can invite them to teach what they know to some of their peers. This personalises learning in two ways.

First, it gives the pupil who has finished a challenging task with which to engage. Teaching requires the manipulation of that which one knows and understands such that this knowledge and understanding can be effectively communicated to others.

Second, it gives pupils who are perhaps struggling with the work extra support. This support will be couched in linguistic codes and social norms with which they are familiar and comfortable. These points stem from the fact that students speak and act in certain ways and these often differ from the speech and actions of adults (including the teacher). Thus, peer teaching can sometimes be easier for students to access than direct instruction from the teacher.

2 Confidence indicators

Confidence indicators are any means through which pupils can communicate to the teacher how confident they are about the work. They can be used by individuals, by small groups or as a whole-class feedback technique (see Chapter 4). For example:

- Thumbs (thumbs up indicates confidence, thumbs down a lack of confidence)
- Fingers (the number of fingers indicates the level of confidence)
- Traffic light cards (red = unconfident; orange = OK; green = confident).

By displaying confidence indicators, pupils can indicate whether they need help. If they do, the teacher can give this (or assign a student to offer support).

An additional benefit of confidence indicators is that, in order to use them, pupils must first think about the work and assess how confident they feel in relation to it. This process involves reflection, active learning and metacognition – all aspects of outstanding learning.

3 Model answers

Model answers may be written by the teacher or students or provided by an exam board, if appropriate. They exemplify an ideal response to a question or task.

Giving pupils model answers to use means giving them expert models which they can copy or imitate. By copy here I do not mean copy verbatim. Rather, I mean copy in the sense that one artist copies the approach of another or a footballer copies a skill shown to them by their coach.

Model answers help students understand what is expected of them as regards a particular piece of work. They also help pupils to access the highest standards in relation to a specific bit of learning; using them helps to open up access across the board, with this then facilitating progress throughout your class.

4 Scrap paper

Scrap paper is a simple tool; one which quickly and easily helps to personalise learning and promote access. It works in two ways.

First, it provides a ready-made extension to our short-term memory. Psychologists have identified the capacity of our short-term memory as seven pieces of information, plus or minus two. This means we are limited in what we can do at any one time.

But, human beings have discovered many ways in which to circumvent this limitation! One of these is the use of scrap paper. Writing things down while we are thinking about them means that we can manipulate more than the seven pieces of information, plus or minus two.

So, for example, if I am engaged in a complex mathematical problem, I can make that problem easier to deal with by transferring some of my thinking out of my short-term memory and onto a piece of scrap paper. Then, voila! My short-term memory is freed up but I can still refer to that which was in there (by looking at the paper).

Second, scrap paper gives us a great place in which to make mistakes. We can use scrap paper for the purposes of trial and error. It is easier to do this than to try to work through myriad trials in our mind. What is more, we can visualise the results of each attempt on the scrap paper, helping us to extract useful information from each mistake we make.

Encouraging your students to use scrap paper means giving them access to the two benefits we have outlined. It means helping them to enhance their cognitive capacities on a short-term basis. This makes accessing the learning easier and makes it more likely that progress will happen.

5 Check sheets

A check sheet is a sheet of A4 or A5 paper containing a list of all the things students need to do:

- To be successful

- To complete a task

- During the course of a lesson

- To reach a certain goal

- Or, to make outstanding progress.

You can make specific check sheets tied to certain lessons or activities. You can also make more general check sheets which can be used again and again.

In either case, the advantage of a check sheet is that it allows students to manage their own learning and, in so doing, take control of the quest for success and progress. This is empowering. It is also motivational and engaging.

Furthermore, you can refer to check sheets during the course of the lesson – either when speaking to the class as a whole or when working one-to-one with students. This means you have a common frame of reference understood by and accessible to both teacher and learners. Therefore, you have a language through which you can discuss learning and progress in the context of the lesson.

Concluding thoughts

That concludes our analysis of Habit Three: Personalising Learning. You will note many connections between what we have here outlined and what we considered in Chapters 4 and 5. This is entirely deliberate and serves to illustrate the fact that the habits intertwine.

It is good this is the case because, while we have sought to delineate the different aspects of classroom practice which contribute to outstanding teaching, the fact remains that when we teach we teach in a holistic sense. That is, we do everything at once.

The consequence of this is that, as you work to embed the habits in your practice over time, you will come to see that they connect together and rely on each other; taken as a whole they present the interwoven reality of what outstanding teaching looks like.

Next up is Habit Four: Building Expertise – to reinforce the point we have just made, you will note that everything we have done so far has been connected to this habit, specifically the part of it connected to pedagogical expertise.

7 Understanding your own expertise

Habit Four: Building Expertise

Outstanding teaching rests on strong foundations. Those foundations are carved from the expertise you possess. Four areas of expertise are of particular importance. We defined these in Chapter 2 and I will remind you of them again here:

- Expertise concerning the subject or subjects you teach
- Expertise concerning the students you teach
- Expertise concerning pedagogy
- Expertise concerning psychology.

In this chapter we will look at each of these categories in turn. In so doing we will explain what expertise in each one encompasses, how this connects to outstanding teaching and what you can do to further develop your skills, knowledge and understanding.

Prior to this we will give a short explanation of what a teacher's expertise is, in general terms, alongside an analysis of why this is important.

What is your expertise and why is it important?

Your expertise is what you know and understand about the job. In relation to outstanding teaching we are talking specifically about what you know and understand about the job in relation to teaching and learning. Of course, other areas of expertise are important but, in this book, it is teaching and learning with which we are concerned.

Any professional finds themselves accorded status in the workplace, and in society more generally, through the expertise they possess. The doctor gains status from knowing about the human body, illness and disease. The lawyer gains status from knowing about the law, its application and its uses.

Teaching differs slightly from most professions because the knowledge and understanding which forms the professional teacher's expertise is drawn from a number of different areas, rather than being primarily focused on one area.

Thus, while it is important for the doctor to have a working knowledge of interpersonal skills, this is subordinated to the central region of their expertise: medicine. It is from the category of medicine that the majority of the doctor's expertise flows – that concerning anatomy, illness, disease, psychology and so forth.

So too with the lawyer. While they need to be familiar with the basics of finance, say, the majority of their professional expertise centres on legal knowledge and legal skills.

In teaching, the basis of expertise is more widely spread – hence the four categories we outline below. This is because teaching is concerned with the content which needs to be taught, the process through which that content is taught, and the relationships and interactions which develop between teacher and student as a consequence of this.

The teacher's expertise is therefore rooted in the classroom; it centres on the process of teaching, which is informed by subject knowledge, pedagogy, psychology and knowledge about individual students.

It is helpful for us to remember this when we are thinking about our jobs and about the meaning of outstanding teaching. This is for two reasons.

First, it is easier to deal with a large concept – such as expertise – by breaking it down into separate categories. This process of analysis turns an unwieldy whole into a series of lighter, easier to manage elements.

Second, we can use the separate categories as lenses through which to look at the work we do day in and day out. In so doing, we can situate the habits we are here outlining, as well as the principles enumerated in the introduction. What is more, we can reflect on our practice in such a way as to identify where we might need to further develop our expertise in order to improve the quality of what we are doing.

A final point to note is that, by having expertise more sharply defined, we are in a position to take control of our own professional development. It is much easier to do this with clearly delineated categories from which to work than it is to simply say: I must develop my expertise. This statement begs the question: Which area of expertise in particular?

As in most areas of life, more closely specifying the nature of things allows us to deal with them more effectively.

And let us begin to deal with the issue of expertise here by stating why the teacher's expertise is so important, in terms of both outstanding teaching and outstanding learning.

As you will have no doubt gathered from the contents of this book up to this point, a teacher who is more knowledgeable about pedagogy – who has a better understanding of what good teaching looks like and the reasoning which underpins it – will always be in a stronger position than a teacher who doesn't.

This is because they will have the means at their disposal to make great learning happen. But also it is because they will have the means through which to make sound decisions and judgements in relation to teaching and learning.

Understanding your own expertise

In the first case, this leads to better lessons being planned, richer activities being used, greater personalisation and so forth. In the second case, this sees cumulative gains being brought to bear as the teacher makes decision after decision which is closer to the ideal course of action in the various situations which arise.

So, for example, an expert teacher will be more likely to make good decisions in the heat of the moment – such as when a pupil is exhibiting poor behaviour in class. Similarly, an expert teacher will be more likely to make good decisions about the type of feedback they give to their pupils, as well as when it should be given and in what terms it should be couched.

This point illustrates one of the key benefits of expertise. Becoming expert means coming to understand what works and why. This knowledge places us in a position from which to deal successfully with situations, whether they are familiar or not. Thus, we see the expert making continued gains over an extended period of time when compared to the amateur (or, even, to the semi-expert).

An example will further reinforce this point.

Consider three chefs, one expert, one good but lacking some expertise and one amateur. In any single situation, there is the possibility that any one of the chefs could produce the best plate of food. However, over the course of twenty or thirty dishes, the expert's superior knowledge and understanding will make itself known and they will produce food which is consistently better than the other two.

The same is true of teaching. An expert teacher will always provide students with better opportunities to make excellent progress than an amateur and, within the profession, more expert teachers are generally likely to facilitate greater progress than their peers.

Before we move on to look at the different areas of expertise, let me make it clear that these areas overlap and interlink. While we have separated them out in order to deal with them more easily, the fact remains that we use them in tandem when operating in the classroom (or outside, when planning and marking).

Your subject

Expertise in terms of your subject differs depending on the Key Stage you are teaching. At primary level, it is expected that you are a generalist; you will need to be expert to some extent in most, if not all, areas of the curriculum. At secondary level, it is expected that you are expert in at least one specific subject.

In both cases, however, the curriculum represents the starting point from which we can gauge, order and manage our expertise. Clearly, we will need to be expert in those areas of the curriculum we are expected to teach.

In addition, outstanding teaching will require you to go beyond that which is set out in the curriculum. The reasons for this are twofold.

First, if you want to continually challenge your students and push their thinking, then you will need to begin with the premise that the curriculum is the main area of learning, but not an exhaustive statement of what can be taught. Thinking in this way means your expertise does not become circumscribed by the curriculum. It also means you will be using further information and ideas to stimulate the minds of your students.

Second, the curriculum never represents a definitive statement regarding an area of learning. Rather, it is an age-dependent, context-specific description of what ought to be learnt, as regards the subject in question, at a particular point in time.

This is important and necessary but does not mean, in and of itself, that this is how matters must end. By looking to go beyond the curriculum in terms of your own expertise you will be better placed to situate, contextualise and explain that knowledge and understanding which has been chosen, with good reason, to form the curriculum. Your students will make better progress as a result.

For example, a History teacher who can explain to their students how the French Revolution influenced conceptions of human rights in nineteenth-century Europe and how this connects to the adoption of the Universal Declaration of Human Rights by the United Nations in 1948 will be better placed to develop their students' understanding of the latter event (which in this example is on the curriculum) than a teacher who can provide no such background.

Outstanding teaching thus relies on:

- An expert knowledge of the curriculum
- Wider knowledge of the subjects which form the curriculum.

The latter is used to inform and improve the teaching of the former.

This expertise also plays an important role in planning.

If we do not have an expert knowledge of the curriculum, it will be harder for us to plan schemes of work and individual lessons which contain rich learning opportunities and which introduce students to new topics in ways which are effective.

If our expertise is limited to the curriculum and does not go beyond this, then our planning risks becoming one-dimensional. By this I mean that it will become heavily reliant on the syllabus provided by the government, developed internally to the school, or provided by an exam board.

While we of course need to cover all the material on such syllabuses, it remains the case that deeper and more effective learning is likely to happen if we can gild and finesse that with which we are provided; not least because the very process of doing this will cause us to think more deeply about the lessons we are constructing and the learning we are asking pupils to do.

Here is another example to demonstrate what we are saying.

A teacher of French who has an outstanding knowledge and understanding of French as a language, who possesses expertise far in advance of that required to make sense of and teach the curriculum, will be able to plan lessons which take advantage of this expertise and which present students with deeper and richer learning opportunities.

This is on top of the fact that they will be able to make use of their additional expertise in lessons, while they are interacting with students, assessing their learning, modelling, explaining, asking questions and so on.

Subject expertise thus falls into two categories, both of which are important to outstanding teaching and both of which we need to develop if we are to ensure our students make the best progress possible.

There are many ways through which we can achieve this end.

An obvious one is reading.

Reading books about the subject or subjects you teach will help you to learn more about them. So too will watching documentaries, reading relevant magazines and newspaper articles and researching topics online.

Further study can provide you with enhanced expertise. If you undertake formal qualifications, this can improve your CV as well.

An often overlooked route is first-hand experience. For example, a Spanish teacher who spends time in Spain, a PE teacher who receives coaching to improve their running, or a Religious Studies teacher who visits places of worship connected to different religions.

A supplementary benefit of first-hand experience is that there is often the opportunity to talk to experts connected to the field in question. Taking the three examples above, the Spanish teacher could discuss grammar with native speakers, the PE teacher could talk about physiology with the coach and the Religious Studies teacher could discuss the nature of Jewish religious belief with a rabbi.

Colleagues can also be a good port of call for the development of subject knowledge expertise. This is particularly true if you work with people who are already specialists or who have a specialism which is different from yours.

Subject associations offer another means through which to enhance your knowledge base, as do online forums and websites connected to the subject about which you teach. Websites such as www.tes.co.uk/resources (by far the best teaching resources website around) contain resources shared by teachers and organisations. These often provide additional knowledge and understanding and have usually passed through a sieve of quality first.

Understanding your own expertise

Organisations which deal with a particular area of study usually have websites which are fruitful repositories of useful information. So, for example, the Imperial War Museum website could help a History teacher to develop their expertise and the Amnesty International website could do the same for Citizenship teachers.

We can see then that it is possible to develop one's subject knowledge expertise via a number of different routes.

The key is to set out with the intention of learning – with the intention of broadening and deepening your knowledge and understanding. This will help you to take advantage of every opportunity to further improve your expertise. It will also help you to think like an outstanding learner and to model the habits of outstanding learning for your pupils.

Your students

There is a reason why many supply teachers have a hard time of it in the classroom – through no fault of their own, they don't know the students.

Being parachuted in without any prior knowledge of who the pupils are, where they are at and what they know makes life difficult.

The flipside of this is that becoming an expert about your students – who they are, their strengths and weaknesses, the way in which they behave, how they respond to praise, what motivates them and how they feel about learning – can have a huge effect on the degree of progress you are able to facilitate.

In many cases, becoming an expert about your students can transform attitudes and perceptions in the classroom – both yours and those of your students.

It is easier to become expert in this area as a primary school teacher, given as how you get to spend an extended period of time with a single class. In secondary school, things are a little trickier – we might only see some of the students we teach once a week (or even once a fortnight if the school has a two-week timetable).

Either way, the importance of becoming an expert about your students cannot be underestimated – nor can the benefits which stem from this.

Expertise in this area covers the following, though this list is not exhaustive:

- Prior attainment

- Personality

- Attitude to learning

- Behaviour both inside and outside lessons

- Strengths and weaknesses

- Reading age

- Any special educational needs

- Whether or not they speak English as a first language

- Target grades

- Knowledge and understanding of the subject

- General cognitive abilities

- Whether they are on free school meals or not (as this group of students tend to underperform nationally relative to their peers)

- Whether they are on the pupil premium register or not (for the same reasons as those just given)

- Relationships with other teachers and students

- Quality of written and verbal communication

- Motivation.

We could go on. Students are multifaceted and unique, just like every other human being.

While the extent of the expertise we need to acquire might at first sight seem off-putting, do not be disheartened. Much of the list concerns things we automatically pick up on anyway.

Understanding your own expertise

Before we look at ways in which you can become an expert about your students, let us outline the connection between this expertise and outstanding teaching.

As we have noted in the preceding chapters (and specifically Chapter 6), outstanding teaching is personalised and tied to the needs of your students. As a result of this, it allows pupils to make the best progress possible.

The more information we have about students – the more expert we are about their learning, their attitudes and behaviour – the better we can adapt what we do to meet their needs and to give them the very best chance of being successful.

In short, if we have a high degree of expertise about our students, we will be much better placed to raise achievement across the board.

To illustrate this point, consider how difficult it can be to facilitate outstanding learning right at the beginning of the year, when you have a new class or a series of new classes. In those first few weeks it is possible to teach outstandingly well, but we all know that greater progress will be made further down the line when we have come to know our new students.

This is in part down to the development of familiarity and the building of rapport. But these two things are themselves constituents of the expertise we develop concerning our pupils.

So how can we develop this expertise?

Well, a number of ways suggest themselves.

First, in relation to learning, there is everything we outlined in Chapter 4. There, we looked at various ways in which you can elicit information from your students. All these methods contribute to your building up of expertise about your pupils.

In addition, we can make use of many of the methods there described – such as listening, observing, talking and questioning – in order to gain information about things which sit as a supplement to learning. These include personalities, attitudes, relationships to other students and general dispositions, among others.

You can also use questioning to discover more about pupils' hobbies and interests. This can be excellent information to use to build rapport. I remember one student I taught who was reluctant to ever do any writing. When, by chance, I found out he supported the Italian football team Juventus, everything was changed for evermore! The rapport we established led to him becoming a prolific writer (or, at least, deciding that he would write in my lessons from that point onwards).

Colleagues are usually a good source of information about students. You can talk to teaching colleagues, form tutors, pastoral leaders and support staff (if appropriate) to find out more about individual pupils. If a student has a special educational need, you should speak to your school's special educational needs coordinator (SENCO).

Another avenue to explore is parents. These are the people who know the children you teach best! You can talk to parents in school, over the phone or at parents' evening. In the case of students who exhibit negative behaviour, it is often useful to speak to parents early on, not only so as to get them on-side and supportive, but also to see if they can provide an idea of why the pupil is behaving in this manner.

You can find out information about your students through your school's data systems as well. Many schools use database software such as SIMS to record attendance, behaviour and much else besides. Looking through the information stored in such a program means gaining a good insight into a student's wider experience of and performance at school.

There are also less direct ways through which to find out about students. For example, you might see pupils you teach at break or lunchtime. This can give you an insight into their character as well as their friendship groups. After-school clubs give another insight, as does participation in activities such as peer-mentoring or school council.

Finally, and to reiterate, never forget that every lesson you have with your students is an opportunity to find out about them, to develop your expertise and to build a clearer picture of who they are and what they can do, such that you might use this information to help them make the best progress possible.

Pedagogy

Pedagogy is the art and craft of teaching. It is the non-identical twin of subject knowledge. One without the other cuts it, but only up to a point. The two need to be hand-in-hand, working together, joined in unison by a common bond, if we are to consistently deliver outstanding teaching.

This is why some academics who have unrivalled subject knowledge are not necessarily good teachers. It is also why excellent pedagogues without subject knowledge so often find themselves swimming around in search of something to teach.

Outstanding teachers marry their subject knowledge expertise with their pedagogical expertise. These two elements of professional ability sit together. They then marry up with expertise regarding students and psychology so as to make the most effective mix.

Expert pedagogy encompasses a range of things. Obviously it includes everything in this book and centres on consistent deployment of the seven habits here outlined (as well as sound understanding of the nine underlying principles first detailed).

It will be to our benefit if we turn this general statement into something more precise. This will provide us with an analytical reference point for the book as a whole and a specific description of the constituents of expert pedagogy.

So, here is a list with which we can work. Expert pedagogy consists of:

- Understanding of what learning is and what progress looks like in the subject(s) you teach.
- Knowledge of a wide range of activities suitable for use in lesson planning – this includes starter, main and plenary activities.
- Understanding of the roles and purposes of assessment, including assessment for learning.

- Understanding of how to personalise learning through the three stages of teaching – planning, teaching and marking.

- Knowledge of different approaches to teaching and lesson planning, including the ways in which these influence how learning happens.

- Knowledge of literacy, its constituents, the fundamental role it plays in learning and ways in which to improve literacy levels.

- Specific strategies, activities and techniques which engage and motivate students, helping them to learn.

The list is not exhaustive but it does cover the majority of that which one needs to know in order to have a high degree of expertise regarding pedagogy.

If a teacher is not an expert in pedagogy, a number of problems arise in relation to outstanding teaching.

First, they risk failing to maximise the progress they are able to facilitate in their classes. This is because they will not have the tools available through which to assess, plan and teach as effectively as they otherwise might.

Second, they are likely to find teaching harder, therefore diminishing the personal return they get from doing the job. This is because they will find themselves regularly experiencing a disconnection between what they want to happen and what actually ends up happening in their lessons.

Third, it is likely they will be unable to take full advantage of any other experience they have – whether this relates to their subject, to psychology, to their students or to all three.

This is because pedagogy is the means through which we put the other expertise into practice. It is the chief area of expertise in the sense that it orders and structures the teaching we do and the learning we facilitate.

A lack of pedagogical knowledge will prevent us from creating and delivering lessons which do what we mean them to do: make learning happen.

Fortunately, there are many ways through which we can grow and improve our pedagogical knowledge.

Understanding your own expertise

We can read books such as this one – books which present us with information and ideas about successful pedagogical practice. In the bibliography you will find various other titles I would recommend; these will help you to further develop your understanding.

We can also read educational research conducted by academics. While the information contained therein is not strictly pedagogical, what it does offer us is evidence and theory on which to base our pedagogy.

Professional development courses can be another route through which to develop our pedagogical expertise. A number of organisations run these around the country, including private providers and local authorities. Most schools also run their own sessions. Some schools do this on a regular basis; others do it only during training days.

Higher education courses such as postgraduate certificates and master's degrees are another option, though these are often expensive. It may be that your school has a training budget containing money which can be put towards course fees.

Observing colleagues is another means through which to develop your pedagogy. If you know of colleagues who are highly thought of or who are known for facilitating great progress from their students, go and observe them teach.

This point leads on to a related one. Talking to colleagues about teaching and learning can give you a good insight into different ideas and approaches as well as helping you to reflect on your own practice.

Reflection in general is an excellent means through which to refine and develop your pedagogical expertise. Personally, I regularly reflect on the impact and efficacy of the methods I use when teaching. I do this both after lessons and during; the latter approach allows you to actively attend to the immediate effects your actions and planning have, both in terms of your students and in relation to the learning in which they engage.

Joint reflection can open your mind to different ways of thinking. It can also offer suggestions and ideas which you haven't considered yourself. This type of reflection can arise naturally within a conversation you have with colleagues or it can be contrived by having a colleague observe you and then following this up with an in-depth conversation.

A more formal manifestation of this approach is mentoring. This is where you work with a more experienced colleague to focus on developing specific parts of your practice. The mentor's role is to offer guidance and support such that you are able to make the kind of progress and development which would be hard to achieve on your own.

Schools tend to assign mentors to newly qualified teachers. If you are further on in your career, don't despair! You can always ask someone to be your mentor and then decide with them how the process will work and what you both want to get out of it.

A less formal cousin of mentoring is coaching. Coaching sees teachers working together in pairs or trios in order to help each other develop solutions to pedagogical problems. Where mentoring involves a more senior colleague advising and guiding a junior colleague, coaching sees teachers working as equals to try to think through problems and issues.

The internet is awash with blogs, articles and websites devoted to teaching and learning. Some of these offer excellent advice, ideas and suggestions; some do not. As with much of the online world, you will need to apply a critical filter to the materials you find.

Speaking of materials, websites on which teachers share resources (such as the peerless www.tes.co.uk/resources, which we mentioned previously) can offer plenty of interesting, helpful and, at times, brilliant ideas about how to improve your practice. These come wrapped up within the resources which colleagues throughout the country (and the world) share.

In terms of my materials, I would direct you to my own website once again – www.mikegershon.com – which contains a collection of free electronic guides to different areas of classroom practice.

These are also available for free through the TES website, where they have proved popular.

The final means through which to develop your pedagogical expertise is your students. This falls into two categories. In the first instance, we can ask our students what they think about our lessons – whether they feel they are effective, what they like, what they would change and so on. Many teachers are loath to do this and, if you don't feel comfortable with it, you might choose to give it a miss.

However, some teachers find it an extremely useful self-evaluation tool which helps them to improve the quality, efficacy and relevance of what they do. In the end, the choice is, and must be, yours.

In the second instance, we have the results which stem from our teaching – the actual progress which students make. While this cannot improve our pedagogical expertise on its own, the information provides us with an insight into whether what we are doing is working or not. From there we can identify whether we need to look more critically at what we are doing and, potentially, change things in order to improve the rate of progress in our classrooms.

Overall, it is fair to say that outstanding teachers take a keen interest in their own pedagogy. They remain critical, open and reflective, desire to learn and develop and do not see their current knowledge and understanding as fixed. It is no coincidence that all these features closely mesh with those habits outlined in Chapter 3.

Psychology

Expertise in psychology encompasses two different areas for the outstanding teacher. On the one hand, we have knowledge and understanding of the scientific findings of psychological research. On the other hand, we have practical knowledge of human psychology – that concerning the interactions and communication we have and experience every day. This is emotional intelligence.

We will look at these two areas in turn.

Psychology in the scientific sense has much to teach us as classroom practitioners. It gives us insights into how the brain works, how the mind operates (if, indeed, the two can be thought of as separate), the nature of personality, ways of learning, thought processes and so on.

Developing a familiarity with some of the basics of psychology is extremely useful for any teacher. This familiarity helps one to understand and interpret some of what goes on in the classroom. It also helps the teacher to create and plan lessons which fit well with the strengths and limitations of the human mind.

So, for example, you will remember that when we talked about scrap paper as a differentiation tool in Chapter 6, included in this discussion was an explanation of how the device can expand the capacity of one's short-term memory.

This is an example of bringing the insights of psychology to bear in a practical sense in the classroom.

Research into memory has given us an understanding of the general capacities we possess in this field. Having this information as part of our general knowledge allows us to use it when planning and teaching.

So, for example, if we see a student who is struggling to manipulate a large amount of data, we might say to them: 'Write some of the data down and put it to one side. Deal with the rest and then come back to it.' Such a comment would be predicated on our understanding of the inherent limitations of the human mind.

Not having at least a basic understanding of some areas of psychology will put the teacher at a disadvantage. While this disadvantage may not be great, it is still an issue which can easily be rectified, bringing benefits to the teacher and to their students.

Rectification is a simple process. Get hold of an undergraduate psychology textbook, or a psychology textbook aimed at teachers or educators, and read some or all of it.

Understanding your own expertise

I would suggest paying particular attention to the areas of learning theory, memory and motivation. You will find reading suggestions in the bibliography.

A final point to note about psychology is that the insights of cognitive psychology have played a big role in the development of learning theory and educational practice over the last half-century or so. One of the most influential theorists in this field is Lev Vygotsky. His books *Mind in Society* (1978) and *Thought and Language* (1986) are well worth investigating as part of any wider engagement with psychological research and theory connected to teaching and learning.

Emotional intelligence is our second area of psychological expertise.

This can be defined as the ability we possess to read the emotions of others, to adapt and mould our behaviour so as to fit with or respond to these, and the extent to which we can manage our own emotions.

So, for example, a teacher who lacks emotional intelligence may struggle to defuse or avoid conflict with certain students. This will probably be because they struggle to read the signals given off by these pupils, to control and direct their own emotions, and to shape their behaviour so as to take account of the emotional element inherent to many interactions.

Fortunately, emotional intelligence can be learned and developed.

Three routes are open to you: reading, observation and reflection.

Reading involves seeking out relevant books on or connected to the topic. Here is a selection I would suggest:

- *Emotional Intelligence: Why it can matter more than IQ,* Daniel Goleman (1996)
- *How to Win Friends and Influence People,* Dale Carnegie (2006)
- *The Chimp Paradox,* Dr Steve Peters (2012)
- *Emotional Intelligence Pocketbook,* Margaret Chapman (2011)
- *Meditations,* Marcus Aurelius (2006)

Books one and four deal directly with the subject of emotional intelligence. Book two gives you practical strategies you can use to positively influence others – and thereby successfully manage the emotional content of interactions. Books three and five present you with different means through which to think about the mind and the roles emotions play in our lives.

Observation involves paying close attention to your own emotions as well as to the behaviour, words and body language of others. If you do not do this already, it may prove difficult at first. Here, you must be persistent. Continuing to observe, reflecting on these observations and then reconsidering them in the light of what behaviour, thinking, speech or actions follow will aid you in your attempts to better understand and manage your own emotions and the emotions of your students.

Reflection connects to observation but can also stand alone.

Reflecting on your own emotions and the thoughts, actions and behaviours to which these lead will help you develop a more nuanced understanding of what emotions are and how they work. This, in turn, should make it easier for you to manage and control your emotions in the classroom so as to create positive results.

Similarly, reflecting on the emotional content of lessons, including the emotions students in your class exhibit, will help you become more familiar with these. This will place you in a stronger position to respond to and deal with these emotions effectively in the future.

For example, a conflict may develop in one of your lessons between you and a student. Reflection will help you think about the emotional cues which led to this conflict. It will also help you assess what warning signs preceded the conflict itself.

You can then use this knowledge to inform your decision-making in the future. The next time you observe similar warning signs, you can look to defuse or mitigate the situation. Thus, you will be in a better position to stop conflict developing.

In one sense then, the development of emotional intelligence is very much connected to trial and error. Instead of viewing negative incidents in the classroom as frustrating, we should see them as learning opportunities. Using them in this way means lessening the chance that they will happen again in the future.

It is also a simple means through which to transform something negative into something positive.

Concluding thoughts

That concludes our chapter on expertise. Running throughout everything we have said is the following point:

> Outstanding teachers continue to learn, and actively seek out learning opportunities, throughout their careers. This helps them to continue developing their expertise. It also helps them to model a growth mindset – one which sees knowledge and understanding as malleable and open to change; something which can be developed through the individual's own efforts.

And, as you will remember, that is a habit of outstanding learning; something we want to be modelling for our pupils wherever possible.

8 Leading your students

Habit Five: Leading Learning

Leadership means standing up and taking charge.

It means helping students get to places they can't or won't go themselves.

In the classroom, you need to be the leader. This doesn't always mean controlling everything or being the centre of attention – leadership also encompasses facilitation and promoting the leadership of others.

Outstanding teaching is invariably found where the teacher acknowledges that their role in the classroom is to be in charge, to know precisely where the class are going and why, and to take students on a journey from the present point to a point in the future where they can do, know and understand more.

Teaching that is not outstanding often lacks any sense of leadership. It sees the teacher failing to acknowledge their own importance: that importance being tied to the fact that they are the only person in a position to decide what will happen, how the learning will take place and where the learning will go.

If the teacher does not take charge and lead their class, a vacuum develops. This can be filled by various things: disengagement; a sense of ennui; low-level disruption; and other familiar obstacles to successful teaching and learning.

One of the most important ways in which the teacher can lead their students is through the promotion and modelling of the habits of outstanding learning outlined in Chapter 3.

In this chapter we will look further at what leadership in the classroom means before drawing out the connections between leadership and both sets of habits – those connected to teaching and those connected to learning.

Within this framework we will pay special attention to two points closely linked to the latter: independent learning and growth mindsets.

What does leading learning mean?

We have defined leadership of learning in general terms. Now we will turn to matters practical.

In this context, leading learning means taking control of planning, teaching and assessment. This includes:

- Being consistently proactive
- Encouraging independence and growth mindsets among your students
- Facilitating progress
- Making and then explaining good decisions.

We have been advocating this approach throughout the book. In one sense, everything we have said so far is concerned with leading learning. This is because outstanding teaching, by its nature, requires the teacher to make the decision that they will be a leader in their own classroom.

Taking control of planning, teaching and assessment means accepting that nobody other than you is responsible for it. This also means accepting that no one but you can make it outstanding.

Really grabbing hold of this idea usually involves making important psychological changes.

No longer can we blame external factors if things go wrong or do not meet our expectations. We cannot apportion responsibility to others; we are in charge and we must do the things necessary to make success happen. If we don't, we only have ourselves to blame.

So, for example, no longer can we say things such as:

- 'There's just too much content to get through.'
- 'You try teaching this class – they're just impossible.'
- 'It's the government's fault.'

All these phrases see us abdicating responsibility. They also see us failing to believe that our actions can make a difference and that, through learning and growing, we can overcome any setbacks we encounter.

We are not here suggesting that we become blind to the reality of events. Rather, we are saying that leadership involves altering how we interpret and respond to these things.

We need to be able to respond with positivity, action, analysis and a belief that our targeted efforts can have a significant and lasting impact. If we do not believe this, then we are not being leaders. This will make it much harder for us to be outstanding teachers. It will also make it much harder for us to raise achievement and secure great progress across the board.

Here we will look at various ways through which you can take control of your planning, teaching and assessment so as to lead the learning of all your students (of course, much else of what we have said in the book ties in to this as well).

Planning: set out your goals

In order to lead you need to have a clear sense of where you are going. This will give you a purpose; it will animate and inform your actions and the choices you make.

Leaders identify the future they want to achieve and then communicate this future – this vision – to those they are leading.

In the context of the classroom, this involves identifying what it is you want to achieve with the class or classes you teach.

You need to provide an answer to the question: What goal or what goals are we working towards?

This may vary from class to class. It may vary from term to term. But defining a goal is important because it allows you to create in your own mind a sense of what the future looks like.

Once in possession of this image you can aim for it and you can share it with your students.

If you do not have a clear sense of where you want to go – of the goal or goals you have for your students and your teaching – then it will be much harder for you to successfully lead the learning in your classroom. This is because you will not have a fixed point which you are working towards and which you can call on to help you when making decisions in the short and medium term.

To give you an example from my own teaching, one of my goals is always to help students to become independent and self-motivated.

Having defined this goal, I can then talk to pupils about it and use it to shape my planning, as well as what I do in the classroom.

If I hadn't clearly identified this goal, I would find myself in a position whereby I could not lead the learning of my pupils anywhere near as well. The problem would be that I wouldn't have a clear understanding of where I wanted them to go. Therefore, I wouldn't be able to make things clear for them or be able to plan and teach as effectively.

Defining your goals involves sitting down and reflecting on what you want to achieve with the pupils you teach. It means specifying the kind of progress you want them to make and getting straight in your mind what you expect this to look like. You can then use this information to help you to lead their learning.

Planning: define what success will look like

With your goals set out, you now need to define what success will look like. This involves identifying what students will need to do, understand or show in order to successfully meet your goals.

This is about stating how you will know that your goals have been successfully met.

As with that mentioned above, the purpose here is to provide yourself with definite views about where you want to take your learners and what it will look like when you get there. By doing this you give yourself the means through which to make good decisions. You will also have clear and relevant information you can communicate to your pupils.

We will use an example to show how this plays out in practice.

Let us imagine we have decided one of our goals is to help pupils become independent. This is a general goal and fits in with the advice given in the previous section.

We now take this goal and analyse it in order to say specifically what success will look like. We define the following:

- Pupils will feel confident trying to solve problems first themselves before asking for help.
- Students will develop their own ideas about the work and follow these through.
- Pupils will be able to get on with tasks with minimal assistance, leaving the teacher free to push their thinking that bit further.

You will note that we have taken our goal and broken it down into precise, practical elements. This allows us to do two important things.

First, we can use these elements as guiding lights taking us towards the wider goal. Thus, we can call on them when we are planning, teaching and when we are assessing students' learning.

Second, we can use them when communicating our vision to pupils. This means that we can not only explain to students where we want to take them in relation to their learning, but we can also state explicitly what they will need to do in order to be successful on this journey.

This will help pupils to understand the goals you are setting for the learning. It will also help you to lead this learning more effectively.

Having defined what success looks like, you can then ensure that you provide students with the right kind of opportunities to be successful. This way, you will be using your prior analysis to shape your planning and teaching such that it matches your longer-term aims.

This is what leading is all about – connecting together the bigger picture (your goals) with the smaller pictures (what success looks like) which need to be fulfilled if the vision is to be realised.

Big picture without smaller pictures does not work. Nor does smaller pictures without a big picture. In the first case, we have an end goal but no means to get there. In the second case, we have the means but nothing through which to direct these.

All this further reinforces the point that successful leadership of learning always involves an understanding of where you want pupils to go (goals/vision) and what they need to do to get there (what success looks like).

Planning: identify how you will respond to problems

Our final technique regarding planning involves identifying how you will respond to problems.

When undertaking any endeavour, it is inevitable that problems will arise. That is the nature of life. Few are the journeys in which nothing detrimental happens or in which nothing gets in our way. In fact, such journeys would probably not result in us learning much or getting very far anyway.

In terms of outstanding teaching, having followed the advice above and identified your goals for learning as well as what success will look like, you must accept that problems will arise during the course of trying to implement this.

Accepting the likelihood of problems does not mean yielding to them. Rather, it means arming yourself in advance with a clear method for dealing with them.

This is like the army general who, before going into battle, identifies all possible things which could go wrong and then develops plans and procedures for dealing with each of these. It is akin to the rugby coach who trains their players in how to respond to the setbacks which might befall them on the pitch when the game is in full swing.

Preparing for problems is an essential part of being a leader.

In the context of the classroom, you will need to do three things.

First, having identified your goals and what success will look like, make a list of all the possible problems which could arise during your lesson planning, your teaching, or during any part of your assessment of students' learning and thinking.

Second, take this list and read it through. For each item on there, think about how you could respond positively so as to ensure that the problem has the smallest possible impact on what you are trying to achieve. Run through in your mind how these responses might play out in practice – What will you do? What will you say? How will you adapt things if your first response doesn't prove successful?

Third, identify any item on the list which has not proved amenable to the combination of critical and creative thinking advocated in the last point. Make a separate note of these items and then spend time attending to the ways in which you could overcome these problems if they arose, mitigate them if necessary or, ideally, avoid them arising in the first place.

This whole process is about rehearsal.

By going over the problems in advance we make ourselves better prepared should they actually arise. This is because we have already worked out ways in which to deal with them.

This is something that great leaders do. It helps them to keep the people they are leading moving towards the end goal in times of trouble.

You can apply the technique to your leadership of learning.

Doing so will increase the chances that you are able to facilitate the progress and achievement you want for your pupils and which

143

you outlined when following the advice given above, in the previous two sections.

Teaching: model high expectations

We move now to look at what you can do in the classroom to lead your students' learning. This section and the following three all focus on practical techniques for use during teaching. They link closely to the points regarding planning we have already made.

Modelling high expectations means doing three things.

First, it involves you communicating your expectations to students throughout the lesson. Second, it means showing pupils what those expectations look like. Third, it includes praising students who have met the expectations, drawing attention to their behaviour and choices and stating why these are good.

This three-pronged approach helps you to embed and then reinforce high expectations in your classroom. In so doing, you will be leading your students, showing them what it is they need to do to be successful.

It is a good idea prior to this process to sit down and identify precisely what your expectations are. While doing this you should think about all aspects of the lesson. This includes the basics such as how students enter the room, how they interact with one another, the kind of language they use, how they talk about themselves and their own abilities, how they respond to you, and anything else which feels relevant.

Working through all this will do two things. First, it will give you a clear sense of what your expectations are and why you have them. Being in possession of this knowledge places you in a strong position; you have identified the specific foundations on which your expectations rest and can thus communicate these to the students you teach.

Second, it allows you to create an image in your mind of what constitutes success in your lessons, in relation to pupil standards. This means you will be in a position to say 'Yes, that is what I expect', or 'No, that isn't good enough', while making direct reference to a defined end you have already identified. If you do not have that end clear in your mind, it becomes much harder to retain consistency across the different judgements you make regarding standards of behaviour.

Modelling high expectations at all times is an important part of leading learning. It shows students what they need to aim for and lets them know what you think they are capable of.

Teaching: create opportunities for independence

Independence means going it alone and trying to do things yourself. It contrasts to dependence which means relying on others to do things for you.

In the classroom, we want our pupils to be independent. The corollary of this fact is that we don't want them to be dependent – either on us or on their peers. If they are, then they are not learning how to take control of matters and do things for themselves.

Creating opportunities for independence means finding periods in your lessons during which pupils can work on their own or during which they have to figure things out for themselves.

One example would be the use of activities which stimulate this, such as independent writing, paired problem-solving (in which both students are expected to contribute) and answering a series of questions in your book before sharing and discussing these answers with a peer.

Another way in which you can promote independence is by taking a step back during the course of teaching and not immediately intervening to help and support students. This is not about removing yourself from the act of teaching. Rather, it is about encouraging pupils to try things themselves first, before turning to you for help. This way, you are teaching them that independence must always come first.

A further example involves setting up a rule which governs student behaviour around independence. So, for example, the rule might be that you will only look at pupil work in a lesson if they can first show you three ways in which they have been independent. Such a rule would encourage students to be independent, helping them to develop this behaviour into a habit which they then continue to exhibit while they are in your classroom.

Independence is one of the hallmarks of outstanding learning. It signals a student who is engaged in their work, believes that they can make a difference to what happens, and who is thinking actively about the learning they are doing.

While it can be difficult at times to take a step back in the classroom and let pupils run things as they see fit, the benefits of this are usually significant. It is almost a case of acknowledging any concern or unease you may feel but then ignoring this and letting pupils take control anyway; which, in the longer term, will be much to their benefit.

Teaching: praise leadership, processes and targeted effort

We mentioned praise before, in relation to high expectations. Here we return to the idea in a little more depth.

Praise is a powerful teaching tool. It reinforces behaviour, signalling to students that what they have done is good and should be repeated. In this sense, praise helps to condition or habituate pupils into certain ways of acting.

Given this fact, we ought to focus on praising those things which we feel will contribute to the development of outstanding learning, as defined in Chapter 3.

The three areas I would pay most attention to here are leadership, processes and targeted effort. We will look at each one in turn.

Leadership in this context means students taking control of their own learning, showing others the way, taking charge of group or paired work and doing things which benefit their own learning as well as the learning of other students in the class.

There is a close connection here to independence and the points previously raised.

Praising leadership will reinforce these behaviours, in the minds of both the students who are doing them and any pupils who observe the praise been given. In the latter case, these students will learn vicariously; they will see what it is that attracts praise, internalise this knowledge and then use it to inform their own choices and actions.

Processes are the things pupils do in order to learn. They contrast to products, which are the end results of students' learning. So, for example, if we set a task in which the aim is to create a leaflet illustrating our knowledge and understanding of gravity, the leaflet is the product and all the thinking and actions we do to create this are the processes.

It is processes which are the constituents of learning. Products are simply the end results. If we praise products, then we are suggesting that the finished result is the thing. But this is not actually true.

It is the learning which is the thing, as we well know. Yet it is only by praising the processes that we can be sure we are actively reinforcing the good elements of learning which have taken place. Praising the product will reinforce the idea that the end result defines what learning has happened. It does not. Rather, it is the processes which lead up to this which are the reality of learning in and of themselves.

And when it comes to processes, students can be most successful by exerting targeted effort. This means they focus their efforts on something specific which connects to their learning, rather than just attempting to follow the general, unspecific dictum of 'trying harder'.

You can indicate to pupils what they should target their efforts on, or you can ask them to critically reflect so as to identify something suitable themselves. Either way, the purpose is to focus their minds and to ensure the effort they put in is underpinned by a clear aim. Praising targeted effort will help to encourage its use and reinforce students' understanding of it as a good thing.

Teaching: communicate where you are going and how you will get there

As we have noted, leaders identify the future they want and then do the things necessary to get there. In the case of the classroom, one of the necessary things is communicating to students where you and they are going and how exactly you will get there.

You can pass this information on in a number of ways:

- By talking to the class as a whole
- Through talking to students individually, in pairs or in groups
- By opening up success criteria
- Through the targets you set
- Through the praise you give
- By explaining your vision and your aims to students
- By talking in terms of outstanding teaching and outstanding learning – what they mean and what they look like.

In all these cases the purpose is the same – to help students understand what it is you want them to do and where it is this will end up taking them.

Communicating where you are going and how you will get there means binding pupils to your vision and giving them the language through which to think and talk about that. It also means giving them a clear idea of what is happening in your classroom on a wider scale – in the longer term; the underlying point behind everything you and they are doing.

If you do not communicate where you are going and how you will get there, then it will be much more difficult for you to lead the learning in your classroom. This is because you will not be guiding pupils into the future and providing them with the tools they need to get to the future you have identified.

Instead, everything will move along regardless, travelling forwards without a keen sense of where that journey is leading.

One technique you might like to try involves spending five to ten minutes at the start of every half-term reminding your pupils about where you and they are going, what it will mean to get there and how far you have come already. Returning to these themes on a regular basis will help you remain focused on them. It will also help keep your pupils on track; they will be better placed to follow your lead and make the progress you want them to make.

Assessment: connect assessment to the habits of outstanding learning

Assessment is the third area through which we can lead the learning of our students. This involves using assessment as a means to guide your pupils forward to the kind of future you want to create in your classroom. We will look at three ways in which you can do this, the first of which involves connecting assessment to the habits of outstanding learning.

When constructing formal assessments, take account of the habits we outlined in Chapter 3. Doing this will allow you to shape the questions and tasks you set so they fit closely to those habits. This means the assessments will both promote the habits and provide you with appropriate information you can use to judge whether or not students are successfully embedding the habits in what they do.

You should make direct reference to the habits when providing formative feedback (see Chapter 4). This involves referring to them in the context of strengths and in relation to the targets students need to implement in order to improve.

Here, we are using the mechanism of formative feedback to provide pupils with information about what they are doing well and what they need to do to get better, in relation to the habits of outstanding learning.

These two approaches serve to intertwine assessment and the cultivation of the habits of outstanding learning.

In a sense, this is a subtle means through which to lead the learning of your students. Without explicitly stating it, you are gently pushing them in directions they might not go themselves. This helps to secure the kind of learning you want to see in your classroom, simply and effectively.

It is also possible to derive cumulative gains from this approach. By continually providing formative feedback tied to the habits of outstanding learning, you will be able to create a cycle of continuous improvement. This will see pupils building on what they have already done so as to get ever closer to the ideal of outstanding learning.

Again, this demonstrates how the approach involves you leading pupils to where you want them to go through the choices you make and the things you do in relation to assessment.

Assessment: emphasise learning from mistakes

One of the most important aspects of outstanding learning is being able to learn from your mistakes. If you can't do this, you miss opportunities to get better, to develop your understanding and to learn from that which didn't work when you tried it.

We know that many students struggle to embrace mistakes. Instead of seeing them as learning opportunities they view them as problems to be avoided or negative experiences which need to be swiftly put to one side – at least, in part, so the ego and the sense of self can be protected.

We can use assessment to promote the idea of growth mindsets. That is, perceptions concerning learning wherein the student believes that they can develop and grow their own knowledge and understanding; and that the process of doing this is directly connected to the actions the student takes.

Here are three simple techniques through which to lead learning in this way.

1 Mistake-centred formative feedback

When providing students with formative feedback – whether this is written or verbal – pay attention to the mistakes they have made. Paint these mistakes in a positive light and show how pupils can use them to improve their work.

For example:

> Chloe, this is an excellent attempt to recreate Van Gogh's Sunflowers. I can see from the attention to detail that you have focused a great deal of effort on trying to get this right. Using the wrong colour for the sunflower leaves is great because it has let you see how you need to trial mixes on scrap paper before putting them onto the canvas. You're now in a position to use this knowledge again in the future – let me know what happens when you do.

I appreciate this rendering of speech is not completely lifelike. Nonetheless, it serves to illustrate the point that you can use your formative feedback to lead students' learning and encourage them to see mistakes in a positive light.

2 Mistakes in formal assessments

When you set a formal assessment, explain to pupils that marks are available for evidence of trial and error, mistakes or 'working out'. Specify how many marks are available and what, exactly, these will be awarded for.

In some Maths examinations, this is already the case.

Here, we are showing our students that errors and mistakes are a good thing – an important and natural part of our thinking and any learning that we do.

When you mark pupils' work, assess the evidence of trial and error, mistakes or 'working out' they provide. Refer to this in your formative feedback and mention the benefits it has brought.

With this technique, you might also like to develop a discussion with your pupils in which they critically analyse the role mistakes, trial and error and 'working out' played in the successful completion of the assessment.

3 Mistake and learning log

Create an A4 template containing two columns. Column A should be labelled 'mistakes' and Column B should be labelled 'what I learned from the mistake'.

Print enough copies for every student in your class. Hand these out and ask pupils to stick them in the front of their books.

Whenever students complete an assessment, invite them afterwards to reflect on the mistakes they made and to discuss these thoughts with a partner. Having done this, they should note down the mistakes they identified on their sheet as well as what they learned from these.

You might like to provide two opportunities for reflection and recording per assessment – one directly after and one when students have received your formative feedback. This will help them to embrace mistakes they have identified, as well as ones you have identified.

One of the great benefits of this approach is that it allows pupils to track their learning over time and to clearly visualise how they have continually learned from their mistakes. This sends out a powerful message concerning the nature of progress and the role played by failure.

What is more, you can use these sheets and the notes students have made on them as a stimulus for discussion during the course of future lessons. These discussions could involve the whole class, pairs or they could centre on you and a single pupil talking through the benefits to which mistakes give rise.

The final point to note regarding the mistake and learning log is that it can act as a powerful exemplar for future groups of students. So, for example, you might take a copy of one of your pupil's logs from last year and show this to your new class in the first week of term. This will help them to understand what the log is all about, how you are expecting them to use it and the ultimate results which flow from it.

Assessment: empower your pupils

Our final assessment-based strategy for leading learning involves empowering your pupils. Empowerment is always to be welcomed in the classroom. It promotes independence, helps students to perceive themselves as actors who can influence events through their own agency and gives a sense of control (which is, in itself, energising and motivational).

Here are three ways through which you can use assessment to empower your pupils.

1 Formative feedback

Formative feedback is empowering because it shows students what they need to do to succeed. It also indicates why this is likely to lead to success. Pupils who receive formative feedback find themselves in a position to make progress under their own steam, as a direct result of their own volition.

This is empowering. We know from our own experience that having the keys to success in our grasp makes us feel positive about the task in hand. Everybody wants to achieve success. Knowing what is necessary to do this is a great thing. Providing this information for your pupils is a good way through which to empower them and, by extension, lead their learning.

2 Provide time and space in which students can make mistakes

Imagine you are learning how to cook. The chef who is teaching you is standing behind your back, looking over your shoulder. Every time they see something going wrong they step in and correct you. Sometimes this even involves them taking over and doing the cooking for you.

For example, they watch you whisking eggs and see that you are not doing this as well as you could. So, they take the whisk out of your hands, pick up the bowl and do it themselves, saying something like: 'Watch me. This is how you do it.'

Such an approach in no way empowers the student. In fact, it does the opposite. It makes them dependent, uncertain of their own actions and reluctant to try in case they get things wrong.

In the classroom, you should provide time and space in which students can make mistakes. This will be empowering. Especially if tied to the type of positive formative feedback outlined above.

In relation to assessment, you can provide time and space in which students can make mistakes by carefully planning formal assessments, by not jumping in too early to offer help or advice based on any information you have elicited, and by presenting assessments as learning opportunities (for you and the students) as opposed to high-stakes summaries of what has been learned.

3 Peer- and self-assessment

We looked at peer- and self-assessment in Chapter 4. There, we explained how they are a useful means through which to open up success criteria for our students.

Both activity types are also inherently empowering. This is because they help pupils to understand and apply the criteria which are being used to judge their work. Through this, students come to feel like they are involved in the process of assessment – that they are active participants in the marking and improvement of their own work (as well as the work of others).

These benefits are best achieved if you use peer- and self-assessment consistently over an extended period of time. Through doing this you will be leading the learning of your students, continually habituating them into conceiving of themselves as responsible for their own progress and development.

Concluding thoughts

That concludes our focus on leadership of learning. You will note that much of what we have said connects to other areas of the book. It is fair to say that everything here suggested is, in essence, tied up with you acting as a leader in your own classroom. This chapter has been about drawing that point out and making it clear, as well as providing specific means through which you can turn leadership of learning into a reality.

9 Unpicking literacy

Habit Six: The Lens of Literacy

Literacy is central to nearly all the learning which goes on in school. As such, we must pay it close attention if we want to teach outstandingly well. Failure to consider literacy – failure to take account of it as part of our planning, teaching and assessment – means it will be harder for our students to make the best progress possible.

In this chapter we will first examine the nature of literacy before connecting this to how we plan, teach and assess. Then, we will provide a range of practical strategies, activities and techniques you can use to promote high-quality speaking, listening, reading and writing in all your lessons.

Speaking, listening, reading and writing

These are the constituents of literacy:

Speaking, listening, reading and writing.

It is these which make up literacy. Therefore, the term, while referring to a thing in itself (the extent to which someone is literate), signifies four separate abilities.

Someone who is highly literate is able to speak, listen, read and write to a high level. They can manipulate, understand, use and decode language in each of these ways.

While this is all fairly obvious, it is worth mentioning because the use of the term 'literacy' in an educational context has sometimes proved problematic. This is because it has been applied in different settings without due regard to its meaning, leading teachers to question precisely what is being referred to when it is invoked.

So, let us be clear. When we are talking about developing Habit Six: The Lens of Literacy, we are talking about:

- Paying close attention to the speaking, listening, reading and writing which goes on in your classroom.

- Thinking carefully about how to maximise the opportunities students have to improve their speaking, listening, reading and writing abilities.

- Referring to these four areas in the context of assessment – in terms of both the kind of assessment opportunities you create and the kind of feedback you give (closely connected to Chapter 4).

- Personalising learning in the context of these four areas wherever possible (linked to Chapter 6).

- Leading students in forming positive habits which will help them to develop their literacy skills, such as learning from mistakes and embracing challenge (connected to Chapters 3 and 8).

This makes clearer what we mean when we use the term 'literacy', as well as what we mean when we say 'the lens of literacy'.

To sum up, here we are concerned with looking at the literacy element of our lessons, how we can attend to this, how we can improve it and how we can help students to make great progress in relation to it.

Literacy in every lesson

Literacy is central to nearly every lesson for a number of reasons.

First, the majority of the curriculum focuses on developing knowledge and understanding based around words. Words are the means through which we communicate, store and develop knowledge. They are the building blocks of language and being able to decode and manipulate them is vitally important if students are to make as much progress as possible.

Nearly all teachers understand these points implicitly. This leads to them doing things in most of their lessons which enhance and help their pupils' literacy development.

However, as we have consistently highlighted through the course of this book, outstanding teaching is not just about doing the things which raise achievement, engage learners and secure progress. It is also about doing these things with a clear understanding of why you are doing them and what effects you expect them to have.

Working in this way is important for two reasons.

First, it is always better to do the right thing for the right reasons than it is to do the right thing without understanding the reasons why. In the latter case, you run two risks. There is the chance that things might start to go wrong without you realising; and there is the possibility that your actions may be influenced by other factors, causing them to change over time.

In both cases, you would not have the means to check that you were still doing what was right.

Second, if we understand the reasons behind our actions, then we can talk to ourselves and others about why we are acting as we are. Through this talk we can further articulate the reasoning and the ideas which animate our decision-making. This helps us to build more solid foundations on which to rest our endeavours. And solid foundations are more likely to last.

So, if we want to be outstanding in the classroom, not only do we need to do things which facilitate the development of high-quality literacy skills, but also we need to underpin our behaviour with clear reasoning as to why we are acting in this way.

And that reasoning is by no means particularly complex.

It pretty much runs as follows.

Being able to read, write, speak and listen effectively means being able to communicate better. This allows students to develop their knowledge and understanding more quickly. It also allows them to access new knowledge and understanding more easily. This raises achievement, helps pupils to experience success, secures progress and, for all three of these reasons, makes lessons more engaging and makes learners more motivated to work hard.

Retaining these thoughts in your mind while planning, teaching and assessing will help you to repeatedly make good choices about literacy – choices which bring great benefits to your students.

For example, they will help you to make good use of the activities, strategies and techniques outlined below. And they will cause you to think about what you can do to facilitate the development of pupils' reading, writing, speaking and listening abilities in every lesson you teach.

Literacy and progress

Paying attention to literacy means increasing the chance that all students in your class make great progress. This is for the reasons outlined above. Here, we present five examples of how this approach might manifest itself in practical terms. These examples link closely to what we looked at in Chapters 4, 5 and 6 (and also retain a tangential connection to Chapters 7 and 8).

1 Eliciting and using information

When eliciting and using information, you can pay specific attention to information which tells you about your students' literacy levels. Some such information is usually recorded in school, independently of lessons (such as pupils' reading ages). Other information can be elicited through all the means outlined in Chapter 4.

Having elicited information about the relative speaking, listening, reading and writing skills of your students, you can then use this to inform your teaching – the activities you use, the questions you ask, the support you give and so on.

For example, you might find out that one of your pupils is verbally articulate but struggles with writing. Armed with this knowledge, you would be able to support them with writing frames, sentence starters, model answers, paragraph structures and much else besides. If you didn't have the information, this might never happen.

2 Assessments

You can construct formal assessments so they contain space in which students can demonstrate their literacy skills. This serves two ends.

First, it provides you with excellent information about pupils' abilities (see the point made above). Second, it serves to structure your teaching so that you take account of the importance of literacy. This is because you will be constructing lessons and individual activities which aim towards the formal assessments you have planned.

Thus, you will be in a position where you cannot help but pay close attention to the role of literacy in your lessons – including the ways in which you can help pupils to improve their abilities.

3 Feedback

Having elicited and used information about students' reading, writing, speaking and listening, as well as developed formal assessments which closely connect to these, you will find yourself in a strong position to offer relevant formative feedback.

This feedback will give pupils the information they need to improve one or more of the elements of literacy.

So, for example, it may be that you observe one of your pupils struggling to summarise in their own (written) words text they have read from a hand-out. You notice the same issue arising out of the formal assessment that you set for your class.

You then use this knowledge to give the student in question a piece of feedback such as the following:

> Abdul, the effort you put in to trying to summarise the reading is excellent; this is really helping you to learn and make progress. To improve, try using bullet points for your summary. This will help you to break up what you are reading, making it easier to put it into your own words.

As you will note, the feedback identifies a strength, praising the process that Abdul is engaging in. It then provides a clear and specific target he can implement to improve his literacy skills.

4 Planning

If we are paying attention to literacy, then we are in a position to plan ways in which to promote and develop reading, writing, speaking and listening skills within our lessons.

So, for example, we might include activities, strategies and techniques such as those outlined later in this chapter.

We can also decide to focus on specific aspects of literacy which are particularly relevant to the class we are teaching. Perhaps the group as a whole struggle to write well, or maybe successful speaking and listening has proved elusive with a particular class. Whatever is the case, we can incorporate a specific literacy focus within our planning.

One example is the use of discussion to precede writing. Doing this means giving students the opportunity to clarify, refine and articulate their thoughts prior to transferring these into the written word. This method involves breaking up the cognitive work – the

161

speaking and listening involved in the discussion is separate from the subsequent writing; this means the development of what students want to say is separate from the process of setting this down on paper, increasing their chances of being successful in both aspects of the enterprise.

5 Personalisation

Clearly, the other four points we have made all include elements of personalisation. In each case, we are doing things which differentiate the learning, making it easier for our students to engage with the work and make progress, both generally and in the specific context of their literacy skills.

There are a couple of other points to note, however, before we move on.

When it comes to literacy and personalisation, we must be aware of the highly specific needs some of our students will possess. Here I am referring to pupils who have a special educational need and those who speak English as an additional language.

In both cases, it may be that students require highly specific, perhaps even specialised, support. You will need to find out what is the case by identifying who in your class is on the SEN register and who speaks English as an additional language (EAL). Having done this, you should then speak to the SEN and EAL coordinators in your school (who are sometimes the same person). They will be able to give you relevant information about the literacy needs of the students in question.

For a range of ways in which to personalise learning for EAL students, see my free resource The EAL Toolkit (available at www.mikegershon.com) and my book *How to Teach EAL Students in the Classroom: The Complete Guide* (2013).

The final point to note about personalisation and literacy is that we cannot do everything at once. Literacy development is a continuous process. For some pupils it can take a long time.

The best approach is to remain persistent in your development of Habit Six: The Lens of Literacy. This will help ensure you are doing everything possible, lesson after lesson, to raise standards of literacy in the classes you teach.

Creating high-quality speaking and listening

We now move on to look at some of the practical strategies, activities and techniques you can use in your classroom. First, we concentrate on speaking and listening.

1 Rephrasing

Ideally, we want students to be using speech in a mature, articulate and accurate manner. Achieving this end takes time. It also requires regular feedback. This can be in the form of specific, targeted comments, more general praise or admonishment, or more ambiguous responses which need to be 'read' by pupils (such as the raising of eyebrows or the crossing of arms).

Rephrasing is an excellent technique through which you can provide immediate, specific feedback to students on their speaking without stopping the flow of the discussion or risking disengagement from a pupil who feels they have been unfairly criticised. Here is an example of how it works:

Student: 'We were doing football yesterday in the park.'
Teacher: 'Super answering of the question. **When you were playing football in the park yesterday**, what happened in the game?'

Note the emboldened text. Here the teacher is rephrasing the pupil's language so as to provide a model of correct usage. The technique is unobtrusive, effective and suitable for use in nearly any situation.

2 Paired discussion

Paired discussion is a great activity you can use in any lesson and at almost any point to facilitate effective and relevant speaking and listening. It simply involves asking students to discuss something with their partner. Here are three examples:

- Discuss your thoughts about the question with your partner.

- When you finish your essay, share it with your partner and take it in turns to discuss the approaches you have used.

- Discuss John's answer with your partner. Focus on how you would develop the answer so that it better meets the success criteria.

As you will note from these examples, the key with paired discussion is to provide pupils with a clear focus. Communicating exactly what it is you want them to discuss is important otherwise the efficacy of the activity will drop.

Paired discussion is particularly good as a prelude to writing. This is because it gives students a chance to clarify, refine and develop their ideas before rendering them in the written word.

3 Expect justification

When making the connection between standards of literacy in general and speaking and listening in particular, it is important to consider the underlying intellectual framework we are seeking to develop.

As pupils become more literate, they increasingly interiorise those aspects which are unique to the written word (don't forget that literacy in our culture is predicated on the written word, even if it also encompasses oracy).

One of the central elements of language with which we are all familiar is justification. Once words become fixed, checkable and comparable to evidence and examples, we expect significantly more advanced degrees of justification than is the case in purely oral societies.

As such, and in order to really maximise the development of literacy through speaking and listening, you should always expect – perhaps even demand! – justification from your students when they are debating, discussing or answering questions.

This expectation will serve two ends. First, it will habituate pupils into providing justification for the claims, opinions and arguments they make. Second, it will convey to students the high esteem in which we as a society hold justification and, therefore, its worthiness as a goal to be pursued.

4 Listening frame

Listening frames help students by doing a little bit of the work for them, therefore allowing them to concentrate on the process of comprehending and analysing what the speaker is saying.

A frame usually consists of a prior delineation of subject matter placed on a sheet of A4 paper with enough space for the student to write down what they pick up about each topic. An example is shown on the following page.

Listening frames can be used in many different settings: as a supplement to discussion; while the teacher is giving a short lecture; in conjunction with a video or audio recording; while students are watching a performance.

Two significant benefits accrue from their use.

First, listening frames help students to listen effectively. They provide a degree of scaffolding which makes the task simpler (meaning, therefore, that they may not be necessary for all pupils) and also present a model of how to listen successfully (from a comprehension/analysis perspective).

Second, they help students to make relevant notes which they can then use in a further task or as part of an ongoing discussion.

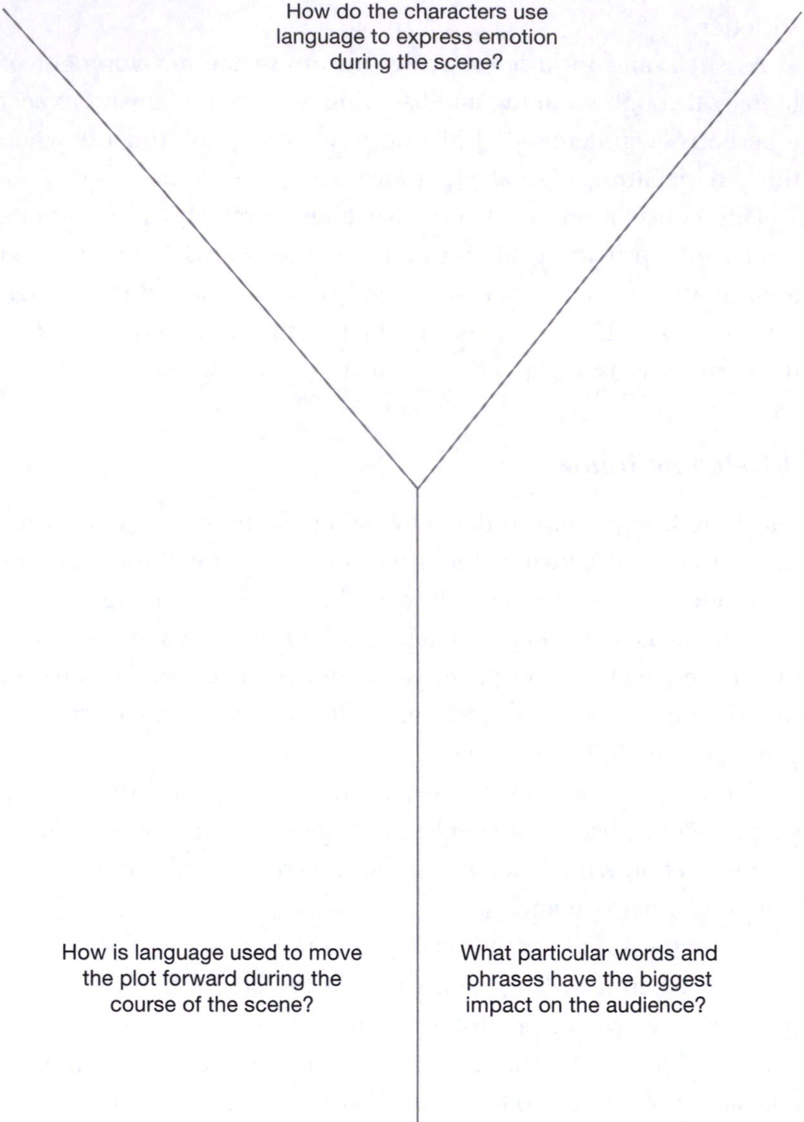

How do the characters use
language to express emotion
during the scene?

How is language used to move
the plot forward during the
course of the scene?

What particular words and
phrases have the biggest
impact on the audience?

Figure 9.1

5 Rehearsal

Repetition helps us to get better. By doing things over and again we become more familiar with them. This is particularly true if we actively engage with the repetition – if we think consciously about the processes we are repeating, as we do them.

Rehearsal is formalised repetition. The formalisation stems from the fact that a rehearsal takes place with a specific end in mind: the performance.

By rehearsing speaking and listening, students are able to improve their skill levels and general abilities.

Rehearsal can be built into activities or it can be standalone. Either way, it should be done with an end in mind. This could be a performance for the whole class, for another pair or for the teacher. Alternatively, the rehearsal could be geared towards a final written performance in which students make use of the work they have done in order to produce a higher-quality piece of text.

An additional point to note is that you can build rehearsal into your lessons simply by asking students to talk to their partners before they share an answer with the whole class.

6 Stimulus material

When it comes to speaking and listening, the best debates and discussions tend to be those in which students are engaged, motivated and working in pursuit of a clear goal (which could be as simple as the desire to make their voice heard on a topic they think is important).

Bearing this in mind, we can see how important it is to have good stimulus material.

The better the stimulus you use to spark up discussion and debate, the more likely that students' speaking and listening will be underpinned by motivation and engagement.

Stimulus material covers anything and everything you use to facilitate speaking and listening. This includes questions, images, objects, videos and statements.

In general, contentious stimulus material works well. This does not mean that all stimulus material has to be deeply controversial, just that it should be open to more than one interpretation (otherwise, what is there to discuss?).

7 Keyword quotas

Keywords are central to every subject on the curriculum. Students with higher literacy levels tend to have a better grasp of these and also tend, as a result, to be more adept at using them.

It can sometimes be the case that pupils shy away from including new keywords in their speech. This is often the result of habit and sometimes caused by a lack of confidence (or fear of failure).

Keyword quotas are a great way to remedy the issue.

During a speaking and listening activity, display a set of keywords connected to the topic on the board. Explain to pupils that everyone must include a certain number of these as part of the speaking they do during the task. This is their keyword quota.

You might even like to give pupils a hand-out containing the keywords so they can cross off the ones they use as they go along.

8 Modelling

You are the biggest learning resource in your classroom. This is in terms of your knowledge and understanding of teaching and your subject but, crucially, also in the more general terms of you as an adult.

You are a model for every pupil you teach. You present actions and behaviours which are there to be copied. This encompasses the physical things you do in the classroom such as how you interact with students and the mental things you do such as solve problems or deal with uncertainty.

An important way in which to develop literacy through speaking and listening therefore involves providing excellent modelling for your pupils.

You can model great speech through your use of language, consistent justification and direct responses to questions.

You can model great listening through your body language, questioning and by paying attention to the detail of what has been said.

And don't be shy in drawing attention to what you are doing. Make a point of indicating to students why what you are doing is good and why, by extension, it is a model which they should follow.

As an aside, you might also like to use specific students in your class who display excellent speaking and listening skills as models for the class to imitate.

9 Speaking and listening rules

Rules regulate behaviour. They provide an external reference point which everyone can understand. This means we can predict with reasonable accuracy that those with whom we are sharing a space or who are engaged in the same activity as us will most likely follow the rules.

In turn, we can predict behaviour fairly well. This makes us feel safe and confident.

If rules are not enforced, perceived as unfair, or varied instead of being fixed, then these benefits may not accrue. Usually, however, this is not the case and the use of rules generates many positives.

Speaking and listening rules will bring the general benefits of rules to bear on the discussions and debates your students have in your classroom. The rules will serve to regulate speaking and listening, promote good behaviour and encourage the development of excellent habits.

You can come up with your own set of speaking and listening rules or you can develop them with your class. In the latter case, this can increase the sense of ownership pupils feel towards the rules.

10 Interviewing

Interviewing is a really nice activity you can use to help students practise and develop their speaking and listening skills. It usually works best at the beginning of a unit of work.

Introduce students to the topic of study. Then, explain that pupils need to develop between six and ten questions (depending on how much time there is available) connected to the topic which they can ask their peers.

Let students work in groups or pairs to develop their questions. To help them, provide some model questions either verbally or displayed on the board.

When everyone in the class has their questions, invite pupils to stand up and start interviewing each other. Set a certain number of interviews which all students need to achieve (five, for example).

When the interviews have been conducted, ask pupils to write a summary outlining their findings and any conclusions they can draw from their research.

You can further develop the activity by:

- Using it as a revision task. In this case, students develop questions which test the knowledge and understanding of their peers. The interview process thus becomes a mini-revision session in which speaking and listening forms the medium through which revision takes place.

- Asking students to produce a more detailed write-up containing an explanation of their method, why they chose their questions and an evaluation of what they would change in the future. This helps pupils to reflect on the speaking and listening they did, as well as the thinking which underpinned this.

Reading and writing

Having considered speaking and listening, we now turn to reading and writing, presenting ten activities, strategies and techniques you can use to support students in your lessons. The first six entries cover writing; the remaining four deal with reading.

1 Writing: paragraph structures

Non-fiction writing consists of three things. The right words in the right sentences, separated out into relevant paragraphs. Fiction writing is a little more complicated because of the role of speech, although we could subsume the separate items of written speech into the category of paragraphs to make life simpler.

Let us not worry about that here though. Instead, we will concentrate on non-fiction writing which forms the bulk of the work pupils do in school (and therefore the main written element of literacy).

Paragraph structures are ways of writing paragraphs. It's as simple as that. Examples include PEE (point; explain; evidence); PEEL (point; explain; evidence; link); and PESEL (point; explain; support; evidence; link).

They help students because they provide a simple structure on which to hang the right words brought together in the right sentences.

As such, they do some of the work for pupils, allowing them to concentrate on the content of their writing. In addition, if used repeatedly, it is likely that students will internalise the structures, thus becoming habituated into an effective style of paragraph construction.

2 Writing: keyword highlighting

Keywords are absolutely essential if one wishes to write well within the conventions of a genre – whether that is the genre of journalism, biomedical science or GCSE Religious Studies.

All areas of thought possess their own keywords. This is the language by which such areas are defined; the means through which people have come to explain and describe the world and ideas through that particular lens of thinking.

The more effectively pupils can use keywords, the better the quality of their writing. This is true across the board.

One way to help students improve their use of keywords is as follows.

Upon completion of a piece of work, give pupils a highlighter pen and ask them to highlight all the keywords they have used. Next, ask them to reflect on whether they have used a sufficient number, whether the ones they have used have been used correctly, and what they could do next time in order to improve their work.

If there is time available, invite students to compare their findings with one or more of their peers. Stress that this process should include pupils looking for examples of excellent usage they can imitate in future work.

3 Writing: planning techniques

Planning makes life easier. It allows us to focus on the minutiae of what we are doing, safe in the knowledge that the big picture has been taken care of. For example, if we plan how to cook a meal, we do not then need to think about the bigger picture while we are doing the cooking. Instead, we can focus on the cooking itself, ensuring we do everything to the standard we desire.

Exactly the same principles apply when it comes to planning and writing. If we plan what we want to write in advance, the actual writing is simpler and easier. This is because we can attend with the full force of our minds to the task in hand (getting the words right) without having our focus torn in two by a subsidiary task (working out what to write about and where it should go in the wider scheme of things).

You can teach your students planning techniques and even insist that they use them as part of their work. One way in which to do this involves giving pupils a success criterion which states something like: 'You must show evidence of having planned your writing in advance.'

Sometimes, pupils can get a bit carried away with planning. They end up writing out half of their work in advance, rather defeating the true purpose of developing a plan. Guard against such situations by stressing the benefits of simple, pared down plans. You could even provide exemplars for pupils to use as guides.

4 Writing: rough rewrite

As more-experienced language users, we appreciate the fact that writing often goes through a series of changes before being presented as a finished product. Students do not necessarily share this understanding.

The key reason writing is redrafted, edited and rewritten is so that it better conveys the author's original intentions. Writing is simply a means of communication, after all. And the point of communication (generally) is to successfully bridge the divide between minds.

Helping pupils to understand the benefits of altering and refining their work is important. If they appreciate these, then they will be more likely to acknowledge the fact that their writing will be better when redrafted, edited or rewritten.

A simple way to introduce the wider notion sees you asking your students to write out their ideas in rough before going on to rewrite these in the form of their finished work. This technique eases pupils into the habit of rewriting, removing some of the sting by classifying the first attempt as 'rough work' or 'work-in-progress'.

Such an approach minimises some of the angst which can arise if we ask students to alter or refine a piece of work they regard as 'finished'.

5 Writing: genre conventions

Every piece of writing we ask students to do is accompanied by some set of specific genre conventions we expect them to meet. Examples include:

173

- Report-writing conventions
- Essay-writing conventions
- Question-answering conventions.

Unless we make students aware of these conventions, we run the risk of setting them up for failure. Without an understanding of what is required to be successful when writing in a particular genre, how can pupils be expected to succeed?

They might succeed, of course. But we can increase the chances of all students succeeding by sharing with them what is required if one is to write well.

For example, we might talk to pupils about how to begin and conclude essays. Or we might press home the importance of including the question in the answer. Or, we might show them an exemplar report before indicating why it is a model of its type.

However you choose to talk about genre conventions to your students, you can be sure that doing so will increase the likelihood that their writing will be both fit for purpose and successful.

6 Writing: good work discussion

As we have noted elsewhere, imitation plays a major role in learning. It is frequently the first staging post on the road to mastery. We watch someone else, read something, look at something and then try to copy it. Eventually we transcend the stage, move on and produce things which can be described as singularly our own, no longer an imitation but nonetheless still historically connected to those first acts of copying.

In terms of writing, examples of good work are great for use as models. Students can look at these, analyse why they are deemed to be good and then seek to imitate elements of them in their own work.

One way in which to bring this process into your lessons is through good work discussions. Divide the class into groups of three. Provide each group with a piece of good written work and a relevant mark-scheme or set of success criteria. Next, ask students to discuss why the work in question can be classed as good. Encourage them to make connections between the writing and the success criteria or mark-scheme.

7 Reading: annotation methods

Successfully annotating a text is a tricky business. It is something which is often overlooked as part of the teaching process. Many of us (me included) are guilty on occasion of failing to give pupils clear guidance on how to effectively annotate.

As a cure for this malaise, let me present three methods you can teach to your students:

- *Highlight key sentences.* Ask pupils to read a piece of text and to highlight what they believe to be the key sentences. You may give specific guidance on what constitutes a key sentence or you may leave it up to students to decide. Indicate that once they have highlighted the relevant sentences, pupils should annotate each one so as to explain why it is important.

- *Connect to three things you already know.* Present pupils with a text and ask them to read it through, looking for three connections they can make to things about which they already know. Having identified three connections, students should annotate each one of these, noting down what the connection is and how the new information is relevant.

- *Ask three questions.* Suggest that students identify three questions they want to ask a text. For example: What is the key message the author is trying to get across? What information here is most important? How does this connect to the topic? Having come up with three questions, pupils can then use these to direct their analysis and the attendant annotation.

8 Reading: summary methods

Here are three summarising methods you can teach your students. Each one will make it easier for them to read and précis texts connected to the topic of study.

- *Bullet points.* Instead of asking pupils to rewrite a piece of text in their own words, ask them to pare it down into a given number of bullet points. Three or five is usually a good number to go with. Bullet points are easier to produce than prose because they represent discrete pieces of information. They are often easier to use subsequently as well for the same reason.

- *Table.* Distilling the essence of a text into a table is a good way through which to summarise the content of that text. Tabulation allows the reader to break a piece of writing down into separate segments and then to store these in a form which is easy to refer to and use.

- *Three-sentence paragraph.* If you would like your students to write summaries in continuous prose, why not make life a little easier for them by inviting them to write one or more three-sentence paragraphs? Each paragraph will need to be concise and focused, emphasising the central features we expect to see in any good summary.

9 Reading: traffic light highlighting

Provide students with a piece of text and ask them to read through it. Next, ask pupils to get into pairs and provide each pair with three highlighter pens: one green, one orange and one red.

Invite pairs to discuss the text. Encourage students to share their thoughts on the writing, focusing on the meaning of the it. Indicate that pupils should aim to discuss any problems, issues, uncertainties or confusion they have with regard to the writing.

Next, students should take the highlighter pens and code the text according to the following system:

Green = I fully understand this.
Orange = I understand some of this, but not all.
Red = I do not understand this.

Upon completion of the highlighting, pupils will be in a position to see exactly what aspects of the text they need to work on (or which aspects they need help with).

10 Reading: clues

When we read texts we know what to look for. This is because we are experienced readers.

When students read texts they may not know what to look for. By giving them clues we can help them on their way. These include:

* Keyword clues (for example, which keywords to look out for)
* Structure clues (where key points are most commonly found)
* Signpost clues (things such as subheadings, emboldened text and quotes, all of which tend to signpost key aspects of a text)
* Prior knowledge clues (things we already know about which form part of the text we are analysing)
* Language clues (specific types of language which signal key information in a given genre).

The clues we give can be specific to the text in question (look out for the words 'cause', 'changes', and 'events') or they can be more general in nature (aim to identify three key points for each individual subheading).

Concluding thoughts

That concludes our chapter on literacy. As you can see, the most important message here is that you should include a focus on

Unpicking literacy

literacy – students' ability to read, write, speak and listen well – in everything you do. This will help you secure great progress through the impact it has on pupils: their skills, their content knowledge and the way in which they can combine these in order to communicate and learn effectively.

Explaining ideas and questioning views

Habit Seven: Creating Clarity and Confusion

Our final habit concerns the communication which takes place in the classroom. This includes teacher–student communication and, to a lesser extent, student–student communication. We will focus on the two most important aspects of this communication: explaining and questioning.

First, we will look at what we mean by the phrase 'creating clarity and confusion'. Then, we will divide the remainder of the chapter roughly in half, focusing first on explaining things and then on effective questioning.

Throughout this second section we will turn our attention to practical strategies you can employ in order to teach outstanding lessons and secure great progress.

Creating clarity and confusion

Clarity and confusion are the two watchwords you can use to inform your communication in the classroom.

By clarity we mean using explanations to help students understand the ideas and information you want to teach them or about which you want them to learn. By confusion we mean using questioning to push students' thinking, helping them to think differently and more deeply about the topics in question. We will look at each of these points in turn, in a little more detail.

Creating clarity is one of the prerequisites of all teaching, not least teaching which is outstanding. Students come to us with a certain amount of knowledge and understanding – about the subject and about the world in general – and it is our job to help them expand and develop this.

In order to access new material – new learning – pupils must be able to understand it. This understanding usually relates to one of two things:

- Understanding what things mean
- Understanding how to do things.

The former concerns content, the latter skills. Both are important, neither can, or do, exist in isolation.

Understanding what things mean usually entails knowing the meaning of words connected to those things. This reflects the central role of literacy in the curriculum, as we noted in the last chapter. Students need to be able to decode the language of a subject before they can do anything with the ideas and information connected to that subject.

Beyond this, there is the need to understand the relationships between different things which words denote. So, for example, a Geography student needs to understand the words 'river' and 'meander' and how these two words are related. Again, the teacher can help with this process. They can explain ideas, or facilitate discovery, such that pupils appreciate the nature of the connections.

Further areas of meaning which pupils need to understand include:

- Relevance
- Interpretations
- Effects
- Degrees and extents
- Causes and consequences.

And more besides, though there is not sufficient space here to go into greater detail.

What we can say, however, is that explanation will nearly always begin with the meaning of words and the relationships between those words (and, therefore, the things those words denote).

To reinforce this point, we will look at an example.

In a Religious Studies lesson we are examining the concept of forgiveness. We know that pupils will have an existing under-standing of this term and that this will be based on their experience of the word (and of forgiveness as an act or thought).

In terms of our teaching, we first need to explain to pupils the meaning of the word in a religious context. This meaning will differ to some extent from the meanings with which they are already familiar.

Next, we need to see how the word relates to other areas of religious thinking. So, for example, we might look at Christian and Islamic conceptions of forgiveness and we might use specific case studies as a way to explain these.

Only at this point would we be ready to go further and start explaining and exploring other aspects of forgiveness – such as its relevance to non-religious people, different interpretations in society, its effect on individuals and groups, and so forth.

All of this serves to illustrate how explanation is always first concerned with doing our groundwork. That is, defining and contextualising words and their meaning for the students we teach.

It is only after we have done this basic groundwork that we can go on to explain things in more detail; or our students can go on to explore them in greater depth.

This process creates clarity. It gives pupils a clear sense of what new ideas and information mean. This learning acts as a basis from which further thought and engagement can take place.

We move now to think about creating confusion.

Confusion means pushing students' thinking. It means using questioning to help pupils think differently about a topic, such that they might come to learn different things about it, develop their thinking on the matter, and know and understand more than was previously the case.

If we do not create deliberate confusion in our classrooms (as opposed to accidental confusion, which is more a function of poor communication), then we cannot be certain our pupils will ever think beyond the basics, or beyond that with which they are most familiar.

So, for example, a student who never has their thinking challenged – who never experiences confusion – will likely continue using and relying on the concepts and categories they developed at quite an early point. While these concepts and categories might be sound, they also might not be. We will only know if we test them. And we do this by asking pupils difficult, thought-provoking questions.

Operating in this way means we are doing a few things with our questioning.

First, we are challenging pupils, causing them to think more deeply than would otherwise be the case. Second, we are showing students that learning is a continuous process. It does not just stop when we have reached a specific point. Third, we are modelling for pupils the fact that confusion is not necessarily a bad thing. If it comes as the precursor to more developed thinking, then it is, in fact, to be welcomed.

We will develop our earlier example to illustrate these points.

Having explained the meaning of forgiveness and how this connects to different religious contexts, we might set our students some work to do around this. For example, an investigative activity in which they examine different religious quotes and then note down to what extent these preach forgiveness.

At this point, the lesson would most likely have been moving along swimmingly and, therefore, it would be the perfect time to sow some confusion!

We might ask questions to the whole class, such as:

- Why might forgiveness be seen as a sign of strength?
- Will religious people always be forgiving and why?

- If forgiveness is such a positive thing, why is it that so many people refuse to forgive? Are they deliberately trying to make life difficult and painful for themselves?

Or, we might talk one-to-one with certain students or groups. In these cases, we could employ some of the differentiation strategies outlined in Chapter 6 to make sure our questions were carefully tailored to the pupils in question.

Whichever approach we took, the purpose would be the same. Having helped students to gain clarity through our initial explanations, we would then look to problematise their understanding by presenting alternative viewpoints, different ideas or provocative questions.

Creating confusion is thus about moving students on from their initial assimilation of new knowledge. It is about introducing shades of grey and encouraging pupils to think more carefully.

In the remainder of this chapter we will look at practical ways through which you can create clarity and confusion in any lesson you teach.

Explaining things

Explaining is one of the core tasks for any teacher. This stems from the fact that the teacher knows or understands something and wants to communicate this knowledge and understanding to their students.

By explaining, the teacher helps pupils to access the knowledge or understanding. Through this, they bring clarity.

Here we will look at twenty ways in which you can explain things to your students.

1 Modelling

Modelling means providing a model which students can look at, imitate, copy and use as a basis for their own work or thinking.

Models can also be internalised. Through this, students come to understand the content of the model.

Frequently, modelling involves the teacher physically modelling something for their pupils. For example, they might show students how they want them to move around the classroom during a group work activity. Or, they might model what excellent speaking and listening looks like.

Modelling can also involve the provision of working models, such as that of a solar system or the digestive system. In this case, the model serves to visually explain that which might be hard to comprehend through words alone.

A final point regarding modelling is that you can use pieces of exemplar work as a model. In this case, students have a piece of work they can copy, imitate or borrow from in order to produce something themselves that is high quality. We look at exemplar work in more detail further on.

2 Examples

Examples contextualise that which is abstract or general. Through this process they make things easier to understand. Here is an example(!):

> Many visitors have criticised the council's decision to charge for entrance to the park **(A)**. For example, one parent who brought her children all the way from Bristol said: 'It's just not on. This makes it too expensive for ordinary families. It's completely unfair.' **(B)**

Here we see how the piece of abstract or general information **(A)** has been contextualised by the example **(B)**. This helps us to better understand **(A)**. It explains it for us, giving us a concrete reference point which embodies the information and demonstrates how it plays out in practice.

Examples are usually verbal, written or visual. In all three cases they provide the audience with an effective, accessible route into understanding. In the classroom, it is good to use examples regularly when you are introducing new material. They are one of the simplest and most useful means through which to develop understanding.

3 Analogies

Analogies are a type of reasoning. They involve us making a comparison wherein we say that one thing is like another thing. Through this process, they help us gain a better understanding of the first thing. Here is an example:

> Leadership is like swimming. You need to keep your head above water so you can see where you're going.

As you will note, analogies take something we know and use that to explain something we don't know (or that we know less about).

In the example, we are using the common experience of swimming to illustrate an important point about leadership.

Analogies bring two great benefits. First, they offer students a way to comprehend that which is new or unfamiliar. They do this by situating the new material in the context of something with which pupils are already familiar. In the above example, leadership (unfamiliar) is compared to swimming (familiar). This helps us to understand a little more about the former through reference to the latter.

Second, they tend to provide strong imagery. This not only aids the development of understanding but also helps students to remember the analogy as well.

The main weakness of analogies is that they can only be stretched so far; beyond that point they will break. In the example above, we can compare leadership to swimming. However, if we pushed this comparison further, it is likely that it would stop working; the fit would not remain.

A good analogy can stay with you for decades; a bad one will quickly be shown up for what it is.

4 Case studies

Case studies are examples writ large. They provide us with a narrative overview of a particular topic through the lens of an individual case.

For example, when studying the effects of pollution from factories, we might exemplify this by using a case study of a nearby factory. Or, when looking at the experiences of refugees, we might do this by looking at case studies of three different people who have been forced to leave the countries in which they live.

Case studies are helpful for two reasons. First, they situate ideas and concepts within stories. As we will see in the next entry, stories are fundamental to human experience and are an excellent way through which to convey information.

Second, case studies make use of individual cases, often involving people. These are usually easier to relate to than general or abstract explanations. This means that students can better understand the ideas in question, being able to make sense of these through a relevant, real-world situation.

5 Stories

Since language first developed, stories have played an integral part in human experience. They are the means through which we make sense of our lives – of the things we do and of the things which happen to us.

We conceptualise the flow of events which constitutes our experience in narrative form. We give our days and the things which make them up a sense of meaning by describing them as stories – with a beginning, a middle and an end.

Many teachers throughout history have used stories to convey their messages – Jesus, Martin Luther King Jr and Gandhi, to name but three. One of the reasons is that an audience can instantly access a story.

Often, they are memorable as well.

These two factors serve to make stories an excellent tool through which to express and explain ideas and information – even those which are highly complex.

In the classroom, you can use stories to contextualise and convey the things you want to teach about.

6 Visual explanations

Visual explanations include diagrams, flow-charts, visual algorithms, graphs and charts, pictures, storyboards and equations. Other methods also exist, many of which I am sure you will be familiar with from your own experiences.

All these explanation types share the fact that they allow learners to see information. Visual presentation offers a different route into knowledge and understanding: one which differs qualitatively from anything based purely on speech or writing.

Visual explanations can be particularly useful for explaining processes, connections, relationships and how things work. This is because they very quickly show information which would take much longer to convey through speech or writing.

The most effective visual explanations are those which are relatively simple. Adding complexity to diagrams, flow-charts and so on takes away from the key benefit they bring; namely, the immediate representation of information, suitable for assimilating in a snapshot. Complexity forces the viewer to engage more closely with the visual explanation, thus making the approach less effective and harder to use.

7 Body language

Body language is rarely able to explain anything on its own – at least not in the context of information and ideas connected to the curriculum (although it can, to some extent, explain emotional states and so forth).

However, body language is an excellent supplement to other types of explanation. So, for example, if you find yourself explaining something verbally to your class, you can add in gestures and facial expressions to help clarify and enhance the meaning of what you say.

Doing this means providing students with additional information about your explanation. They can use this information to decode what you are saying and as a means through which to confirm the content of your message. To get a good sense of effective body language, watch consummate politicians or actors when they are speaking. Here you will find highly effective use of body language as a supplement to spoken messages.

8 Re-explaining

We cannot be certain that pupils will understand our explanations the first time around. That is why it is always worth re-explaining the ideas and information we share with them.

Re-explaining involves going over the same topic but in a slightly different form. So, for example, having used a diagram to explain Brownian motion you might then re-explain this using an example and, on the third occasion, through an analogy.

Re-explaining serves two ends. First, it gives students a second, or third, or fourth chance to come to terms with whatever is at issue. Second, it gives pupils an opportunity to check what they think they have understood against the information provided as part of the re-explanation.

Many students find it helpful to be able to clarify and confirm what they believe they have understood the first time around.

9 Step-by-step

The step-by-step method is an effective way to explain a process:

- *Step One*: Identify the thing you want to explain.
- *Step Two*: Identify the separate elements which constitute the thing in question.

- *Step Three*: Put these elements in order from beginning to end.

- *Step Four*: Go through and make sure you know how you will explain each element.

- *Step Five*: Communicate your step-by-step explanation to your students.

As you will note from this example, the step-by-step approach is a wonderful means through which to break down a process. It allows you to draw out the separate elements and then deal with these one at a time, in order.

As such, the method is superb for making complex processes simple. It is also an excellent means through which to illustrate the logical structure underlying a process.

Finally, a major benefit of the step-by-step approach is that it presents pupils with a method they can take away and use (or simply refer to) again and again.

You will have made use of this approach yourself on a number of occasions: recipes, instruction manuals and map directions, for example.

10 Instructions

Instructions are a way of explaining centring on the communication of what someone else needs to do in order to get something done. We can give instructions through a step-by-step method but we can also give instructions in other ways. Hence why there is a separate entry here.

Instructions are only appropriate as a means of explaining in certain circumstances. The three commonplace examples we called on above – recipes, instruction manuals and map directions – are all examples of situations where the audience needs to be guided through a process which the author understands but they do not.

Similar examples in a school context include: using equipment; using software; and procedures such as checking work before handing it in. As you can no doubt see, at certain times the instructions you give will be step-by-step whereas on other occasions there will be no need to conform to this highly circumscribed method.

11 Crib sheets

Crib sheets provide students with basic information about a topic, process or idea. A classic example comes from Science or Maths in the form of a page of paper containing formulae which pupils might need to use during the course of an exercise.

Crib sheets explain certain important aspects of a topic. Students can use them as support devices. This relates to the explanations they offer and the use to which pupils can put them while engaging in an activity.

It might be that you hand out crib sheets at the beginning of a topic. This will allow you to help and support pupils while they are getting to grips with the area of study. Further down the line they will be able to put the crib sheets to one side and carry on without them.

12 Doing things in practice

Practice is a great way through which to open up understanding. It is a sort of hands-on, unfolding explanation in which the person who is doing the practising comes to understand the thing in question through the actions in which they engage.

So, for example, while you may stand in front of your class and explain a new activity to them, it probably won't be until they have tried it out for themselves that they will really understand it. The practical experience will allow them to develop an insight into how the activity functions. It is hard to gain such understanding through other means.

Doing things in practice opens up ideas and information in plenty of situations; for some pupils it is an absolutely central aspect of how they learn. For others, abstract manipulation of ideas and information will come more naturally.

13 Antonyms and synonyms

We mentioned these in Chapter 6, where we demonstrated their usefulness in helping to explain new keywords to the pupils we teach.

The same points apply here.

You can use antonyms and synonyms to help students understand new ideas and information. This is because the words they already know become a lens through which to view and unlock the words with which they are not yet familiar.

So, for example, we might explain marmalade by saying that it is synonymous with orange jam. Or, we might explain precipitation by saying it is another word for rainfall.

14 Demonstrating

Demonstrating overlaps with modelling but is by no means identical. This is because demonstrating does not necessarily involve the student copying what they see. For example, a demonstration of the reactivity of potassium will only ever encompass the teacher demonstrating this to their students (because it is too dangerous for the pupils to do themselves). The demonstration serves to explain the abstract point by providing relevant experience.

Demonstrations can be done in person or they can be conveyed through video. You only need to take a cursory glance at YouTube to find a wide range of demonstration videos dealing with various skills and ideas.

15 Assigning meaning

Providing a clear rationale for something means contextualising that thing in terms of what it means and why it ought to be the case. Being able to access such meaning means understanding the thing in question more easily. It also makes remembering it easier as well.

Here's an example:

- Shut the gate on your way out.

- Shut the gate on your way out because last week the milkman left it open and the dog escaped. I found him six hours later in the centre of town digging up one of the municipal flowerbeds.

The first instruction carries little meaning. There is no 'why'.

The second instruction has meaning assigned to it. We have a 'why'. This makes it easier to understand and to remember.

16 Using mistakes

We have been advocating the benefits of mistakes throughout, stressing how they are excellent learning opportunities. This connects, in particular, to Chapter 3 and the habits of outstanding learning.

If we can help our students to embrace mistakes and to see them as a force for good – for learning – then we are onto a winner.

One way to cultivate such a perspective is to use mistakes as an opportunity to explain things to pupils. This explanation will usually centre on why the thing in question is wrong and how thinking about it differently can help you to get to the right answer, or simply to a better answer.

17 Exemplar work

Exemplar work is a model which helps explain to students what constitutes great work in the subject you are teaching. Exemplar material also provides pupils with a means through which to understand information and ideas in context – that is, in the context of school and the classroom.

You can give out examples of exemplar work and ask pupils to analyse these on their own, or you can take the whole class through exemplar work in one go, unlocking the learning points for all students at the same time.

18 Comparison

Comparing one thing to another helps us to explain and understand the thing in question in two particular ways. First, in order to make a comparison we must look at both things in detail. This involves us coming to better understand those things. Second, the act of comparison involves seeing the things in question in a different light – that light being provided by the fact that we view one thing through the lens of the other, and vice versa.

So, for example, if we compare a square to a circle, we first analyse the nature of a square and the nature of a circle before then looking at each from the perspective of the other. All this helps us to better understand both squares and circles.

This holds true for any act of comparison.

19 Role Play

Role play can take one of two forms in the context of explanation.

In the first case, the teacher can use it to explain something to the class. This sees the teacher taking on a role in order to demonstrate how a particular individual might have thought, acted or behaved.

So, for example, to help explain the behaviour of Gladstone in relation to the Bulgarian Horrors campaign of 1876, the teacher might play the role of the famous prime minister, with students then asking them questions about the issue.

In the second case, students take on roles. Through playing these, they gain an insight into the thoughts, actions and ways of behaving of their particular characters.

So, for example, to help pupils understand what it was like to take part in World War One, we might set up a role-playing activity in which they take on the characters of some of the individuals who were involved in fighting on the front line, working on the home front and reporting on events for a national newspaper.

20 Question and answer

Our final method for explaining is question and answer. This involves the teacher fielding questions from students so as to help develop their understanding of the topic at issue.

Question and answer can be conducted formally, with the teacher taking questions from students in turn, similar to a press conference. It can also be an informal process with different pupils asking the teacher questions one-to-one.

We often see the latter happening when pupils want more information – frequently in terms of clarification and elaboration – about an activity or about what the teacher expects them to do.

Effective questioning – creating confusion

We move now to look at effective questioning. Here we are concerned with how you can create confusion in your class; how you can problematise student thinking, causing pupils to look again at that which has become familiar.

Good questioning is conducted with a clear end in mind. In our case, that end is stretching and challenging pupils' thinking. If we do not have a clear end in mind, we risk asking questions which are unproductive, inconsistent or not suitably connected to the matter in hand.

Once we have our end in mind, we can shape our questions accordingly. This helps us to keep focused and to build up a sense of momentum, which will further press the thinking of our students.

Here we present seven techniques you can use in order to ask great questions (and don't forget that you can adapt and develop questioning techniques mentioned in earlier chapters as well, such as Socratic questioning, concrete to abstract questioning and Bloom's-based questioning).

1 Might

The word 'might' makes knowledge provisional. As such, it opens up thinking and encourages students to look into the possibilities surrounding a topic. Here is an example:

- What is the best way to approach this problem?
- What might be the best way to approach this problem?

The second question will result in better thinking and discussion than the first. This is because it provides scope for exploration and alternative perspectives. Thus, the teacher will be in a position to say things such as: 'Ah, but that might also mean . . . '

Using the word 'might' is a simple way to ask more effective questions. These questions will encourage answers which are discursive, predicated on reason and also open to further questioning (as a natural result of the type of discussion which develops). This is harder to achieve with questions which do not contain the word.

2 Open vs closed

In general, open questions are better for sowing seeds of confusion and opening up pupils' thinking. This is because they do not circumscribe the topic at issue. Instead, they provide a way into thought and discussion – one which can lead to many different paths and possible responses.

You can ask open questions at any point during a lesson – whether you are speaking to the whole class, to individual students or to groups of pupils. You can also use open questions as the basis for tasks. In terms of the thinking pupils do, similar benefits will accrue here.

Of course, closed questions need to be used on many occasions. Using open questions wherever possible, though, will help you raise the level of thinking taking place in your classroom.

3 What if . . .

'What if . . . ' questions are provocative. Not in the sense that they are confrontational or contentious, but in the sense that they provoke creative thinking. Here are some examples:

- What if Britain had never had an empire?
- What if the water cycle worked more quickly?
- What if Hamlet had been more chilled out?

In each case, we are using the question stem to recast and provoke the thinking that pupils are doing. This helps to develop that thinking, making it more nuanced and more subtle. 'What if . . . ' questions encourage students to re-examine their ideas about a topic. In so doing, they broaden out and deepen that thought.

Take the first question of the three above as an example. Asking this question means getting students to think differently about the British Empire. It means they have to re-examine their conceptions, pulling apart those things they might otherwise have taken for granted. This leads to far better thinking all round.

4 Show me, tell me, convince me

This is a technique you can use to push students' thinking until they have worked sufficiently hard to persuade you that a certain thing ought to be accepted as the case.

Begin by asking a pupil to show you something. For example: Show me your answer to whether or not Britain should join the Euro.

Then, ask them to explain that thing to you. For example: Can you tell me why you have given that answer? Can you also tell me what that answer would mean for Britain and the countries already in the Eurozone?

Finally, ask them to convince you that their answer is right. For example: But what about the implications for inflation? Can you convince me that your answer has taken account of these?

Here we see how the method works. It starts off gently before getting progressively more challenging. By the end, the student is having to work really hard to convince the teacher that their ideas are sound and should be accepted as such.

You can use this method when working one-to-one with students or when talking to a group of pupils. In the latter case, you can invite students to support one another. This creates a nice atmosphere in which a playful 'battle' develops between teacher (non-believer) and the group (who want to convert the teacher).

5 Conceptual questioning

Concepts refer to ideas. Courage is a concept. So is love. We might also say we have things such as the concept of a table. This does not refer to physical manifestations of tables but, rather, to the general notion of what a table is.

As such, concepts are abstract and non-physical in nature. They are not out there in the world, ready to touch. While we might see someone being courageous, or we might identify courage in someone's character, we cannot pick up or touch courage in the same way that we can a chair.

For all these reasons, conceptual questioning is challenging. Questions based around concepts require students to think in an abstract sense. They demand that pupils engage with ideas and think carefully about these. This is difficult.

Here are some examples of conceptual questions:

- Is it right to deny people medical treatment? (The concepts of right and wrong)

- What does greed mean in the context of the play? (The concept of greed)

- Why might combustion be unlikely in these three scenarios? (The concept of combustion – a concept which is closer to the physical world but which is still, nonetheless, a concept)

In each case, pupils will have to do heavy intellectual labour in order to provide an answer. This is what we want! Great progress and learning will be the result.

6 Role Playing

Here we are thinking about the roles the teacher can play when they are asking questions. These roles include:

- Devil's Advocate (where they hold antithetical, unlikely or hard-to-defend positions)
- Neutral Judge (where they hold no position)
- Committed Participant (where they take a standpoint and then argue from it)
- Slippery Customer (where their views are hard to nail down)
- Flip-Flopper (where they keep changing their minds)
- Philosopher (where they take on the role of Socrates, using the Socratic questioning styles outlined earlier)
- Cross-examiner (where they play the role of prosecuting counsel so as to probe and challenge students' thinking).

In each of these cases, taking on a role gives the teacher a means through which to behave in a different manner to usual. This, in turn, allows the teacher to ask questions and provoke thinking which they might not otherwise have been able to do.

7 Varying the subject matter

Varying the subject matter of your questions helps ensure you explore different ideas and perspectives with your students. It is easy to fall into habits of thinking in the classroom which may lead you to ask questions which are mostly of a certain type or overly concerned with certain issues.

Varying the subject matter of your questions will help to avoid such situations arising. This will then work to stretch and develop your students' thinking.

Student questioning

The final point to make in this, our penultimate chapter, connects to the questions students ask each other.

At the beginning of the chapter we indicated that we would attend to student–student communication as well as to teacher–student communication, in the context of creating confusion.

Everything we have outlined above can be applied to the way in which students communicate with each other in the classroom. Modelling the various questioning styles and drawing pupils' attention to these is an excellent way through which to encourage the development of penetrating questioning as part of your students' communication.

During discussion activities, you might like to highlight a particular questioning technique and then ask students to apply this as part of their efforts.

Alternatively, you might construct a wall display entitled 'What makes a good question?' and then refer to this when pupils are engaged in discussion.

Both of these techniques allude to the same fact: giving students a great model to imitate and then drawing attention to this model is one of the best methods through which to promote high-quality student–student questioning and communication.

Of course, praising that which is good in this context (applying the same principle as we outlined earlier) will also help to engender high-quality interactions.

Concluding thoughts

And so we come to the end of the chapter and to the end of our seven habits of outstanding teaching. All that remains is for us to draw our journey to a conclusion – and we will do that next.

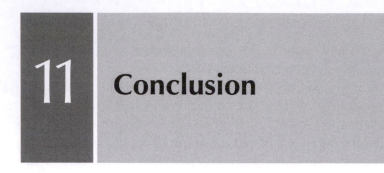

11 Conclusion

So there we have it, the habits of outstanding teaching, supplemented by the habits of outstanding learning.

Everything you need to make learning happen, to secure great progress, to raise achievement and to engage the students you teach.

Everything you need to be outstanding in the classroom.

Who do you want to be?

This is the question you need to ask yourself on a regular basis. In the classroom, who do you want to be?

If you want to be an outstanding teacher, and I'm sure you do, then you need to answer this question every week and remind yourself that this is your goal and that this is what you have set out to achieve – for yourself, for your students and for your school.

Positively visualising yourself as an outstanding teacher will help you to become outstanding. This will provide a picture in your mind you can work towards.

To make that picture a reality, you know what you need to do – put the habits into action, day in and day out, as you are planning, teaching and assessing.

Developing and changing yourself isn't always easy. You need to be persistent. You need to stick at it. You need to acknowledge the successes you have and learn from the mistakes and disappointments, without letting them knock your confidence or damage your sense of self.

This is where the habits really come into their own.

Having the habits to hand means having a point of reference on which you can always call – an anchor to which you can return; which will steady you if things don't go your way, reminding you of what you are trying to achieve and what you need to do to get there.

Outstanding teaching doesn't mean all-singing, all-dancing lessons. Remember that.

It means consistently planning, teaching and assessing to the very best of your ability. It means implementing the ideas outlined in this book and developing your own. It means being open to change and desiring to better yourself through learning, reflection and targeted effort.

These are all things you can do – they are all things which are open and accessible to you.

I think you will do them. I think you will be outstanding in the classroom as a result. I think your students will benefit and I think you will feel, rightly, proud of yourself and what you have achieved.

Your day-to-day: the habits

When it comes to embedding the habits in your daily work, don't try to do too much at once. Attempting to put everything from this book into practice on day one will likely lead you to a dead end. There is too much here to implement overnight.

Instead, pick one or two of the habits and focus on these first. Work at them. Think about how you will embed them in what you do. Concentrate on them for a term. Reflect as you go. Learn from your mistakes. Make use of trial and error. Use it as a means through which to improve your practice gradually but consistently, day after day.

Then, a little further down the line, when the habit or habits on which you have focused first are second nature, move onto a third habit and then a fourth. The whole process might take six months or a year. It might take longer.

That's OK. Becoming outstanding at anything doesn't happen straight away. And remember, we're not concerned with some one-off, fly-by-night outstanding here. What we're focused on is consistently outstanding teaching. Teaching which never drops below a certain level – which always hits the mark; raising achievement, securing progress and engaging students regardless of what day it is or of what the circumstances are.

Your lessons: the habits

In your lessons, pay attention to the habits you are working on – and pay attention to the habits of outstanding learning.

This is an obvious point but, sat reading this book in the quiet and sanguine atmosphere of home or the office, it is easy to forget how quickly our attention can be drained away by what happens in the classroom.

Being aware of this and guarding against it will allow you to focus your energies and your attention on promoting and implementing the habits, both in terms of learning and in terms of teaching.

You will be able to make full use of your mind, bringing all your cognitive capacities to bear on the task in hand – the successful embedding of the habits, over time, in your planning, teaching and assessment.

When you are in the classroom, paying attention, be minded to examine what effect the decisions you are making have on the pupils you teach. How do they respond? How do they learn? How do they interact with you, each other, the content and the activities?

You can use all the information you elicit to reflect on, refine and improve what it is you are doing. This will help you to make progress. It will help you to become better and better at what you do.

Embracing mistakes

Throughout the book we have been emphasising this point – in relation both to you and to your students.

Mistakes are learning opportunities. Never forget this. And don't let your pupils forget it either.

If we don't make mistakes, we have far fewer opportunities to learn. Fewer opportunities to learn means a lower chance of making progress. Not making progress means stagnating and failing to achieve our goals (though that failure may in itself be a learning opportunity!).

In teaching, we make mistakes all the time. This is a natural part of the job. It is perhaps true of any job. It's just that, in teaching, these mistakes often manifest themselves in more obvious ways; sometimes causing us significant headaches!

But don't worry. Don't see mistakes as a problem. They're only an issue if we continue making the same mistakes over and again, without learning from them. If that situation develops, then you should be concerned – at least to the extent that you examine what is going on and seek to make changes.

In general, mistakes are an essential part of developing. They will play a significant role in your attempts to embed the habits of outstanding teaching. You might be lucky and manage all the habits without any mistakes whatsoever. If this happens, good on you!

The likelihood is that it won't though. And you will need to use the mistakes you make as tools through which to get closer to the ultimate goal you are aiming for: to be an outstanding teacher every day of your working life.

Of course, it is also true that thinking and acting in this way will be a brilliant model for your students. They will be able to see, first-hand, a growth mindset in action; one which grabs hold of mistakes, embraces them and uses them as a means through which to learn and grow. That will be a powerful experience for them.

Conclusion

Putting a name on success

Let us draw things to a close by putting a name on success.

That is, identify the criteria we need to fulfil if we want to be outstanding in the classroom.

These have been implicit throughout the book, explicit in places. Drawing them together here will give you a reference point to which you can refer as you work towards your goal.

- You need to elicit and use information to shape your teaching, planning and assessment wherever possible.

- You need to plan with progress in mind, such that you might facilitate it within every lesson you teach, for every student you teach.

- You need to differentiate so as to meet the needs of all learners. Doing this will help you to sustain high levels of progress across the board.

- You need to become aware of your own expertise and build on this throughout your time as a teacher.

- You need to lead the learning in your classroom, familiarising students with the habits of outstanding learning, helping them to be independent and promoting growth mindsets.

- You need to think carefully about literacy and what you can do during every lesson to improve students' abilities to read, write, speak and listen effectively.

- You need to create clarity and confusion through your speech, your resources and your questioning.

All in all, you need to embed the habits of outstanding teaching.

Do so, and you will achieve the success you want.

Good luck, keep targeting your effort on the things that matter, keep reflecting and keep embracing mistakes.

I know you're going to do a great job.

Bibliography

Books

Anderson, Lorin W., David R. Krathwohl, Peter W. Airasian and Kathleen A. Cruikshank, *A Taxonomy for Learning, Teaching, and Assessing* (Pearson, 2000)

Aurelius, Marcus, *Meditations* (Penguin Classics, 2006)

Baddeley, Alan D., *Your Memory: A User's Guide* (Prion Books, 1996)

Baddeley, Alan D., *Essentials of Human Memory* (Psychology Press, 1999)

Baddeley, Alan D., Michael W. Eysenck and Michael C. Anderson, *Memory* (Psychology Press, 2009)

Barton, Geoff, *Don't Call it Literacy!* (Routledge, 2012)

Black, Paul, Chris Harrison, Clare Lee, Bethan Marshall and Dylan Wiliam, *Assessment for Learning: Putting it into Practice* (Oxford University Press, 2003)

Black, Paul and Dylan Wiliam, *Inside the Black Box* (GL Assessment Ltd, 1990)

Black, Paul, Chris Harrison, Clare Lee, Bethan Marshall and Dylan Wiliam, *Working Inside the Black Box* (Letts, 1990)

Bloom, Benjamin S. (ed.), *The Taxonomy of Educational Objectives: Book 1 – Cognitive Domain* (Longman Higher Education, 1965)

Bruner, Jerome, *The Culture of Education* (Harvard University Press, 1997)

Bruner, Jerome, *Acts of Meaning* (Harvard University Press, 1992)

Bruner, Jerome, *Actual Minds, Possible Worlds* (Harvard University Press, 1986)

Bibliography

Bruner, Jerome, *Child's Talk: Learning to use Language* (WW Norton & Co, 1983)

Bruner, Jerome, *The Process of Education* (Harvard University Press, 1960)

Carnegie, Dale, *How to Win Friends and Influence People* (Vermilion, 2006)

Chapman, Margaret, *Emotional Intelligence Pocketbook* (Management Pocketbooks, 2011)

Covey, Stephen R., *The 7 Habits of Highly Effective People* (Simon & Schuster, 2004)

Crystal, David, *How Language Works* (Penguin, 2007)

Dewey, John, *Experience and Education* (Pocket Books, 1997)

Donaldson, Margaret, *Children's Minds* (HarperCollins, 1986)

Dweck, Carol, *Mindset: How You Can Fulfil Your Potential* (Robinson, 2012)

Dweck, Carol, *Self-theories: Their Role in Motivation, Personality, and Development* (Psychology Press, 2000)

Eysenck, Michael W. and Mark T. Keane, *Cognitive Psychology: A Student's Handbook* (Psychology Press, 2010)

Gershon, Mike, *50 Quick Ways to Outstanding Teaching* (Bury St Edmunds, 2014)

Gershon, Mike, *50 Quick and Easy Lesson Activities* (Bury St Edmunds, 2014)

Gershon, Mike, *50 Quick and Brilliant Teaching Games* (Bury St Edmunds, 2014)

Gershon, Mike, *50 Quick Ways to Motivate and Engage Your Students* (Bury St Edmunds, 2014)

Gershon, Mike, *50 Quick Ways to Help Your Students Think, Learn and Use Their Brains Brilliantly* (Bury St Edmunds, 2014)

Gershon, Mike, *50 Quick and Brilliant Teaching Techniques* (Bury St Edmunds, 2014)

Gershon, Mike, *50 Quick Ways to Perfect Behaviour Management* (Bury St Edmunds, 2014)

Gershon, Mike, *50 Quick and Brilliant Teaching Ideas* (Bury St Edmunds, 2014)

Gershon, Mike, *50 Quick Ways to Help Your Students Secure A and B Grades at GCSE* (Bury St Edmunds, 2014)

Gershon, Mike, *50 Quick and Easy Ways to Outstanding Group Work* (Bury St Edmunds, 2014)

Gershon, Mike, *50 Quick and Easy Ways to Prepare for Ofsted* (Bury St Edmunds, 2014)

Gershon, Mike, *50 Quick and Easy Ways Leaders can Prepare for Ofsted* (Bury St Edmunds, 2014)

Gershon, Mike, *Teach Now!: History* (Routledge, 2014)

Gershon, Mike, *How to use Assessment for Learning in the Classroom: The Complete Guide* (Bury St Edmunds, 2013)

Gershon, Mike, *How to use Differentiation in the Classroom: The Complete Guide* (Bury St Edmunds, 2013)

Gershon, Mike, *How to use Discussion in the Classroom: The Complete Guide* (Bury St Edmunds, 2013)

Gershon, Mike, *How to Teach EAL Students in the Classroom: The Complete Guide* (Bury St Edmunds, 2013)

Gershon, Mike, *How to use Questioning in the Classroom: The Complete Guide* (Bury St Edmunds, 2013)

Gershon, Mike, *More Secondary Starters and Plenaries* (Bloomsbury Education, 2013)

Gershon, Mike, *Secondary Starters and Plenaries: History* (Bloomsbury Education, 2013)

Gershon, Mike and Barry Hymer, *The Growth Mindset Pocketbook* (Teacher's Pocketbooks, 2014)

Ginnis, Paul, *The Teacher's Toolkit* (Crown House Publishing, 2001)

Goleman, Daniel, *Working with Emotional Intelligence* (Bloomsbury, 1999)

Goleman, Daniel, *Emotional Intelligence: Why it can matter more than IQ* (Bloomsbury, 1996)

Griffith, Andy and Mark Burns, *Outstanding Teaching: Engaging Learners* (Crown House Publishing, 2012)

Gross, Richard, *Psychology: The Science of Mind and Behaviour* (Hodder Education, 2010)

Hattie, John, *Visible Learning for Teachers* (Routledge, 2011)

Hattie, John, *Visible Learning: A Synthesis of Over 800 Meta-Analyses Relating to Achievement* (Routledge, 2008)

Holt, John, *How Children Fail* (DeCapo Press, 1995)

Holt, John, *How Children Learn* (Penguin, 1991)

Illeris, Knud (ed.), *Contemporary Theories of Learning: Learning Theorists . . . In Their Own Words* (Routledge, 2008)

Leman, Patrick, Andy Bremner, Ross D. Parke and Mary Gauvain, *Developmental Psychology* (McGraw-Hill Higher Education, 2012)

Luria, A.R., *The Mind of a Mnemonist: A Little Book about a Vast Memory* (Harvard University Press, 1986)

Bibliography

Ong, Walter, *Orality and Literacy* (30th Anniversary Edition, Routledge, 2012)

Palmer, Joy A. (ed.), *Fifty Modern Thinkers on Education: From Piaget to the Present Day* (Routledge, 2001)

Palmer, Joy A. (ed.), *Fifty Major Thinkers on Education: From Confucius to Dewey* (Taylor & Francis, 2001)

Peters, Steve, *The Chimp Paradox* (Vermilion, 2012)

Petty, Geoff, *Evidence-Based Teaching: A Practical Approach* (Nelson Thornes, 2009)

Petty, Geoff, *Teaching Today: A Practical Guide* (Nelson Thornes, 2009)

Pintrich, P.R., J.R. Meece & D.H. Schunk, *Motivation in Education: Theory, Research, and Applications* (Pearson, 2013)

Plato and J.M. Cooper (ed.), *Complete Works* (Hackett Publishing Co, 1997)

Sacks, Oliver, *The Man Who Mistook His Wife for a Hat* (Picador, 2011)

Smith, Jim and Ian Gilbert, *The Lazy Teacher's Handbook* (Crown House Publishing, 2010)

Vygotsky, Lev, *Thought and Language* (MIT Press, 1986)

Vygotsky, Lev, *Mind in Society* (Harvard University Press, 1978)

Walsh, Bill, with Steve Jamison and Craig Walsh, *The Score Takes Care of Itself: My Philosophy of Leadership* (Portfolio, 2010)

Winnicott, D.W., *Playing and Reality* (Routledge, 2005)

Woolfolk, Anita E., Malcom Hughes and Vivienne Walkup, *Psychology in Education* (Pearson, 2012)

Zimmerman, B.J., Becoming a self-regulated learner: an overview. *Theory into Practice*, 41(2), 64–72 (2002)

Reports

'Improving the impact of teachers on pupil achievement in the UK' – interim findings, The Sutton Trust, September 2011, www.suttontrust. com/researcharchive/improving-impact-teachers-pupil-achievement-uk-interim-findings/

'Teachers Matter: Understanding Teachers' Impact on Student Achievement' – Rand Education report on the impact of teachers, www.rand. org/content/dam/rand/pubs/corporate_pubs/2012/RAND_CP693z1–2012–09.pdf

The Bill and Melinda Gates Foundation report on the measures of effective teaching, www.metproject.org/

Resources

All available at www.mikegershon.com and www.tes.co.uk/mikegershon

Assessment for Learning Toolkit
The Bloom Buster
Challenge Toolkit
The Curriculum Compendium
The Differentiation Deviser
Discussion Toolkit
EAL Toolkit
The Effective Group Work Toolkit
Essay Writing Toolkit
The Ethicist
The Feedback Compendium
Make Your Own AFL Box
Movement Breaks Toolkit
Peer- and Self-Assessment Guide
The Philosophiser
Plenaries on a Plate
The Plenary Producer
The Political Philosophiser
The Starter Generator
The Ultimate Lesson Activity Generator
The What If . . . ? Box
The Whole-Class Feedback Guide

Index

Index